Supporting Children with Multiple Disabilities

2nd Edition

Michael Mednick

continuum

Continuum International Publishing Group

The Tower Building   80 Maiden Lane
11 York Road   Suite 704
SE1 7NX   New York
    NY 10058

www.continuumbooks.com

Cover photography of : Michael Mednick and Shivangi Patel using the Acoustic Bell All photographs, except those of equipment, taken by Michael Mednick.

British Library Cataloguing-in-Publication Data
A catalogue record for this book is available from the British Library

ISBN: 0–8264–9298–3 (Paperback)
      9780826492982

Library of Congress Cataloging-in-Publication Data
A catalog record for this book is available from the Library of Congress.

Typeset by Techbooks Ltd, New Delhi, India
Printed and bound in Great Britain by Bath Press, Bath, England

Contents

Dedication

This book is dedicated to all children with multiple disabilities, who strive to make sense of the world, seeking acceptance, respect and dignity and looking to us to unlock the door to learning.

Acknowledgements

I wish to acknowledge the use of the CAF Directory regarding medical information. I would like to thank Alison Spanner and Jo Brook, who are physiotherapists, for their advice regarding Chapter 7 and Ian Jordan regarding Chapter 4. Thanks are due to Nottingham Rehab Supplies, Kendall Camp Orthopaedic, Assistive Technologies and Mangar International for their generous provision of photographs of their products. Thanks to Lisa Hicks for her plants advice and to Melissa, Leona and Seth May for allowing me to photograph them.

I would like to thank my fellow colleagues for their encouragement and support.

Finally, I would like to thank my wife Liz for her patience, support and willingness to read my drafts. Also I wish to thank my two children, Melody and Catherine, for allowing me time away from them to write this book, and for their understanding and inspiration to help children with multiple disabilities.

Introduction: A Vision and Philosophy for Working with Children with Multiple Disabilities

The inspiration for this book has been the growing demands placed on professionals working with children with multiple disabilities in mainstream schools. The book is designed to foster good practice in special education and to raise pupils' achievements and communication skills.

Everyone has the ability and potential to learn, regardless of their intellectual or physical ability or age. Everyone has the right to be treated with dignity and respect for who they are and what they can do.

It is clear that many children with multiple disabilities lead lives that have huge difficulties and hardships, and it is all too easy to make assumptions about their level of understanding and their future potential. In order to enable them to reach their full potential, our current thinking needs to be challenged and we need to find creative ways of moving towards goals and educational targets, and to bring about change in the lives of these children. Often, however, working towards change for children can involve some element of change for ourselves as professionals. Self-analysis, or looking closely at our own ways of working, is not always an easy or popular thing to do. It is often easier to look at problems in the child rather than at our own inabilities to reach the child.

To increase independence and communication skills we have to find different ways or paths to 'get the message across'. Often this requires us to be patient, open-minded, flexible, passionate, enthusiastic and energetic, and to have the right spirit, aptitude and heart. We need to see the child as one struggling to make sense of the world, with the same potential to learn as everyone else.

Children should be enabled and empowered. Their disability often renders them helpless, without the opportunity to make real choices about what affects them. We need to give them back as much control as possible, even though most tasks require adult intervention and support. In this way they will start to believe in themselves.

As professionals, it is important to work more closely and effectively with parents and to be partners with them. We need to value their contributions, to accept them as part of a support team, and to value their knowledge and expertise in working with their child. It is their legal right to know what is happening to their child and to be fully informed.

The education of children with multiple disabilities is concerned with improving their quality of life and with finding ways to remove or overcome barriers to improving this quality. Children need to explore new territory and to expand the horizons of their lives.

> As Principle 4 of *A New Contract for Welfare: Principles into Practice 1998* states: 'Those who are disabled should get the support they need to lead a fulfilling life with dignity.'

We can't separate children by saying who can and who cannot learn. All are able to learn new skills and this is not age-dependent. We are often poor predictors as to the future potential of a child. Therefore, it is important not to make too many assumptions and to be careful about our expectations and judgements.

Finding the key that will unlock the door to their world and for learning is the challenge that faces us all. We need to enter the child's world in order to bring them into ours. One of the keys is clearly 'Communication'. However, we will soon discover that once we have opened one door, we are faced with another, which requires another key. So the true challenge we face is the opening of a series of doors and finding the right keys to open them. This book will provide the reader with numerous keys to select. Select wisely and doors will be opened for these children. Each key is important if we are to understand and work with the child. In a jigsaw, when all the pieces are in place a beautiful picture is revealed. When all the keys or pieces of intervention are in place, we will see progress, achievement, empowerment and liberation for the child.

Having a true belief and faith in the future potential of children with multiple disabilities is paramount to our vision and inner philosophy of working with them and meeting the challenges that face us.

A number of statements can be put forward to underline progress:

> VISION without ACTION is merely a dream.

In other words, we may have the right vision, motivation and attitude. However, if we do not put this into action and find the keys, it will evaporate and it is likely that the child will make little progress. Alternatevely:

> ACTION without VISION passes the time.

If we have some of the keys but do not hold the right attitudes and passionately believe in the vision, then again progress will be limited.

> VISION with ACTION can change the world.

However, if we have the right attitude and vision and have the right keys and tools to do the job, we can change the world for the child. For me, I want to change the world for each child I support. I want to be a world changer! The challenge is 'Do you want to be a world changer?'

The child with multiple disabilities has many needs. Schools should be aware of these needs and should be able to meet them, so that the children are able to interpret and understand the world they live in. As educational law now clearly indicates, there is a move towards equal opportunities and inclusive education for all pupils, and therefore these children have the right to receive appropriate education alongside their peers. However, due to the number of problems and difficulties these children present, often this does not occur. The reasons for this include: the need for additional funding arrangements; the changes that would have to take place within the mainstream environment (policies, organization, teaching styles); the effects on examination results and league tables; and a belief that true integration is not obtainable.

This book has been written to provide all those working with children with multiple disabilities with a practical framework of reference and support. I hope it will help professionals to empower and enable children to become more independent and active participants in the world. The book also presents an easy-to-read guide to reduce the complexity of issues surrounding the inclusive education for these children. Throughout the book, the child is referred to as 'he', and the professional as 'she'.

Children with multiple disabilities are entitled to be enlightened, empowered and enabled, as are all children. The onus is on us and society to bring this about. Now, as you enter this book, take this premise and philosophy with you.

Now go and explore new frontiers and find creative ways to facilitate a world of understanding for all who are in it!

1 Children with multiple disabilities

Paul has cerebral palsy, light perception and is seven years old. He understands language, although is unable to use spoken words – replying to questions by arm and hand movements for yes and no. He is fully integrated into mainstream primary school. His best friend is Jane, a child of similar age. She reads to him and pushes his wheelchair in the playground. She says that Paul is her boyfriend and loves to kiss him when she has the opportunity to do so. She is proud to tell others that when she grows up she will kiss him whenever she wants to because she hopes to marry him. Paul loves being with her and clearly demonstrates this pleasure. With her, Paul feels accepted and like his other peers. Jane doesn't see Paul as disabled but as her friend.

General facts

Many perceive that lack of physical control and mobility is the main area of difficulty for a person with multiple disabilities; that he is likely to be non-ambulant and a wheelchair user. The facts do not bear this out.

● Only 5% of those with multiple disabilities are wheelchair users.
● Many children with multiple disabilities are not only physically impaired but have a wide range of needs.
● 65% of all visually impaired children have multiple disabilities.
● 50% of all children with cerebral palsy are visually impaired.
● 80% of all learning is based on vision, 13% is based on hearing, and 7% on other senses.

Perceptions and myths

There are various misconceptions and myths in society which have shaped our thoughts and consideration of people with multiple disabilities. Maybe these perceptions have originated within our own family background, or from our experience at school or in the street, or from the media. Whatever the source, wrong perceptions do influence our understanding, our attitudes and our behaviour towards these children in terms of their future potential and their individual rights.

A number of myths exist about people with multiple disabilities:

● They are all wheelchair users.
● They are completely different from other people.
● They were all born that way.
● They have a sixth sense.
● They mainly/only have friends with multiple disabilities.

- They don't care what they look like.
- They don't pursue adventurous outdoor or indoor sports.
- They can't get married or have children.
- They can't have a job.
- They have low expectations.

Clearly not all are wheelchair users. Neither are they completely different from other people. They may be different because they have some obvious difficulties, but who amongst us does not have difficulties?

The difference is that our difficulties are not always visible and obvious, but can be hidden. Not all people with multiple disabilities were born with these difficulties. Some were acquired due to physical deterioration, or through accident.

These children don't have an additional sixth sense – they do not enter the world with anything more than anyone else. However, because of their disabilities they learn to live in the world by relying more on their senses to reach their full potential.

Many people with multiple disabilities have friends who are not disabled. However, many lack, or are denied, the opportunity to develop friendships outside their immediate disability group because of segregation at school and throughout society. People with multiple disabilities **do** care a lot about their appearance. They **do** notice when their mouth or nose is dribbling and they are embarrassed. However, they may lack the confidence, communication, understanding or physical skills to do anything about it.

They do enjoy adventurous sports including skiing, tobogganing, abseiling, canoeing and swimming but some never have the opportunity to do any of these things. Many get married, many have children, and some may also get divorced. Some of them have physically able children, whereas others may not. Some gain purposeful employment and have a wide range of skills and abilities to offer. However, opportunities and access to places of work may not always be forthcoming, despite political will and legislation.

Many have low expectations because others tend to have low expectations of them, which they have to fight to overcome. Others may have low expectations because of the conditioning other people have placed on them.

Population

The population with multiple disabilities:

- is heterogeneous
- has a wide range of ability and disability
- is cross-cultural.

Multiple disability affects male and female alike. However, there are likely to be more females with a disability than males, mainly because of the general population imbalance. It is true to say that certain conditions are gender-linked, whilst others are not. Jeffree, McConkey, and Hewson, (1977) stated that:

'No two children are alike. They vary in their abilities, temperament, interests and needs. Handicapped children are just as individual as anyone else. Indeed we cannot talk of a typical handicapped child. Different handicaps can have very different effects. For example, the effects of blindness are not the same as deafness. The severity of the handicap can also vary. A child's hearing may be partially lost or he may be almost deaf. Also a child may have one predominant handicap or be multiple handicapped. Thus the type, severity and number of handicapping disorders add to the diversity among handicapped children.'

People with multiple disabilities are in many ways the same as all of us. Some of us are good at mathematics while others are not. Some of us enjoy music, others don't. Some of us have greater intellectual capacity than others have. Why shouldn't this be true of people with multiple disabilities? We must be very careful not to project our likes, dislikes and abilities on these children, but instead to allow them to make their own choices. Although these children may have specific difficulties linked to their medical condition, the methods they use to cope with their difficulties are individual and unique. The age of onset of their disabilities and the access to resources and support are all factors that can determine children's ability to understand, to act and to interact in the world. As such a wide range of ability and disability exists within this group, it is very difficult to have specific assumptions and expectations.

People with multiple disabilities come from all walks of life and cultures. However, some conditions are more prevalent in certain cultures. Again, assumptions cannot be made.

Terminology

This section attempts to unpack the question of terminology. The debate and discussion about terminology or labelling has arisen mainly from the need to categorize children, so that their needs and requirements can be understood. There is a wide variety of disabilities and medical conditions, however, and individual children are sometimes given different labels or categorized in different terms by professionals. This has led to much confusion and disagreement. Within certain parameters, all the terms found in books and referred to by professionals can be related to the same homogeneous grouping under the umbrella term of 'people with multiple disabilities'.

This will help us focus more clearly on the general needs of this group of pupils, rather than be bound by terminology.

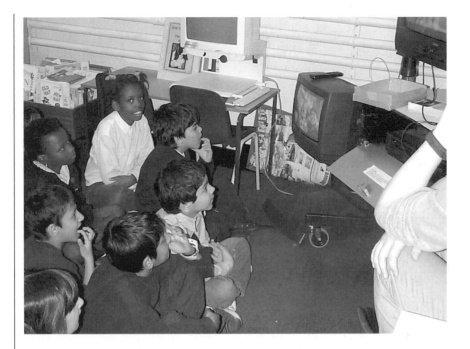

Terms used by professionals

- multiply handicapped
- multi-handicapped
- wheelchair child
- Educationally Subnormal Severe (ESNS)
- handicapped
- Severe Learning Difficulties (SLD)
- acute physical difficulties
- developmentally threatened
- developmentally deprived
- profound and multiple handicapped
- complex needs
- multiple disabilities

There is even confusion over the acronym PMLD:

- Profound and Multiple Learning Difficulties (most commonly used)
- Profound and Multiple Learning Disabilities
- Profound and Moderate Learning Difficulties

Major associations refer to this group as follows:

MHVI (Multiple Handicapped and Visually Impaired) or more recently, MDVI (Multiple Disabled and Visually Impaired)
[*Royal National Institute for the Blind (RNIB)*]

MHHI (Multiple Handicapped and Hearing Impaired) or more recently, MDHI (Multiple Disabled and Hearing Impaired)
[*Royal National Institute for the Deaf (RNID)*]

Deaf-blind became deafblind and now is referred to as Multi-Sensory Impaired (MSI) [*SENSE*]

Derogatory terms

These include:

- cripple
- spastic
- idiot

Parents, peers and child

The parent uses none of the above terms and instead refers to these pupils as 'my child'. Children in school don't use these terms either, they use the child's name or refer to him as 'my friend'. Again, the child doesn't use any of these terms, but refers to himself as 'me'! What do we use?

Definitions

It is clear that there is a wide variety of definitions relating to children with multiple disabilities. However, together, these definitions provide us with a broader frame of reference in truly understanding children with multiple disabilities.

Warren (1984) refers to the term 'multiple handicap' as the coincidence of any of a variety of conditions which would in themselves constitute areas of concern.

In *New Directions* (1985) a child with multiple handicaps is defined as one whose additional disabilities, physical, sensory, mental or behavioural, are severe enough in themselves to interfere with normal development or education. Children with multiple disabilities form a diverse group with many different combinations of disabilities and degrees of severity of handicap.

Cassell (1989) saw these children as suffering from any continuing disability of body, intellect or personality likely to interfere with their normal growth, development and capacity to learn.

Best (1992) asserts that multi-sensory impairment is the most current all-embracing label used to describe a person who has very special and complex needs, particularly relating to the use of information from all senses.

Nielsen (1992) refers to this group as 'developmentally threatened' because they are threatened by developmental delay as a result of their sensory loss and poor physical and motor skills.

McInnes and Treffrey (1984) refer to these children as multi-sensory impaired and as those who receive distorted information due to sensory loss. These children require guidance in sorting out sensory information in a non-distorted way so that they can understand the world.

McInnes and Treffrey (1984) also indicate that the problem is not an additive one, where a variety of conditions can be considered and reviewed in isolation and then put together. They go on to assert that most children with multiple disabilities will need to establish some basic concepts which their mainstream peers have already learned. These children need to establish a sense of self, to learn how to explore the environment, and to learn that they can affect the objects and people around them.

Whatever definition you prefer, what is clear is that the person with multiple disabilities is a bit of all of them and has a number of difficulties that must be considered in a holistic way. In this book I will be using a broader definition and one that will include all of the above. A child with multiple disabilities is a child who has more than one disability, which may include a physical, intellectual, communication, sensory or emotional difficulty. Children with multiple disabilities may fall into all or some of the categories below, which, together, can be remembered as SPICE:

A child with multiple disabilities is a child who has more than one disability, which may include a physical, intellectual, communication, sensory and emotional difficulty

Sensory: difficulty in using and interpreting sensory information, with some inability to sort and to integrate information in such a way that the child can understand the world in an undistorted way.

Physical: this involves a disability in body functions and mobility and includes a varying degree of dependency on physical care.

Intellectual: difficulty in developing concepts and in memory retention.

Communication: a wide range of communications skills will exist in this group, including a variety of non-verbal and verbal communication.

Emotional and psychological: possible difficulties with self-esteem, personality and unacceptable behaviours (e.g. self-mutilation, head banging and rocking).

Meeting people with multiple disabilities

Wyman (1986) describes the entire life of a child with multiple disabilities as being affected by the approach that people have to his needs. If the child is seen as one who needs to be protected against all danger, he is likely to be nurtured in a cocoon of sympathetic emotion. The child will then behave as he is expected to behave: handicapped, limited and probably under-achieving and passive. However, if the child is seen as a person first and foremost regardless of his disabilities, then he will learn, grow and mature. Disabilities will affect the *way* a child learns, but he will learn if given the opportunity – how much and how fast is difficult to forecast.

The difficulties that a child with multiple disabilities will face in making sense of his world are often of such enormity that it is only too easy to forget that he is a human being, and not a robot to be programmed into fulfilling certain goals. Put yourself in the child's place. It is easy to know that the child has multiple disabilities; it is far more difficult to remember, and to take account of, his normal needs in everyday situations.

The basic principles to remember are:

1 Behave normally.
2 Do not avoid people with multiple disabilities.
3 Treat them as you would treat other people.
4 Don't be fearful or nervous.
5 Avoid situations that deny them participation and access.
6 Be sensitive to their needs.
7 Encourage independence and access.
8 Don't assume anything.

Key Points
- Every child matters – have the right vision, philosophy and the world can be changed for that child.
- Find the key(s) that will unlock the door of learning.
- Widen your understanding of the child with multiple disabilities by smashing any myths and misperceptions you may hold.
- Do not narrow your pursuit for the truth by limiting your research as a result of terminology.
- Widen your definition and see all children who have multiple disabilities as children who have more than one disability, which may include physical, intellectual, communication, sensory and emotional difficulty.
- Behave normally and relax when you meet people with disabilities and assume nothing. Be open-minded and you may be pleasantly surprised.

---

2 | Possible problems

John is seven years old and has osteopetrosis and optic atrophy. He is registered blind, having only light perception in his right eye and poor vision in his left eye. He can only read print which is very large and it is likely that John will learn to read Braille in the near future. He has a basic understanding of language and responds appropriately to questions. He expresses his preferences on a wide range of subjects. He was educated in a special school for children with severe to moderate learning difficulties, but for the last two years has been educated in a mainstream school. His parents have always wanted him to be educated in mainstream education, but were denied this opportunity due to the lack of resources in his LEA. When his family moved into another LEA, their views were accepted and he was provided with a place in an inclusive school. He has been in this school with full-time support for the last eighteen months. John can now read simple books with a developing understanding of phonic skills and he can write simple sentences independently. John can make and record simple computations. Before entering mainstream education he had none of these skills. His confidence has grown tremendously and he is often involved in 'horse-play' with his peers. He is an ardent supporter of Liverpool Football Club.

Disorders and delays

Motor difficulties

Many children with multiple disabilities have either hypotonia (floppiness) or hypertonia (stiffness) or are hypotonic (mixture of both floppiness and stiffness) most tend to be hypotonic. However, like us, the flexibility of their body is related to their emotional and behavioural state. If we are anxious, our movements become more hypertonic. Hypotonic movements are more prevalent when we are tired. This is also true for these children, and their movements can become more difficult to control when they are tired or anxious.

The major problem that many have to overcome is the ability to gain control over their own body movements and to reduce involuntary motor responses. Some may need to find alternative ways to overcome and compensate for a physical palsy down one side of their body or within specific limbs.

Poor social and communication skills

Many children lack the ability or opportunity to communicate with others in a meaningful way because of their motor dysfunction and lack of speech. Some children with multiple disabilities communicate in ways that are not readily interpreted as 'mainstream' because the children are non-verbal. These communication methods range from controlled reflexes, breathing patterns, and hand and arm movements, to the use of objects, signing and vocal responses. As these methods of communication are not always consistently recognized and reinforced, children can have extreme difficulty in establishing and maintaining interpersonal relationships. It is only when their methods of communication are accepted that meaningful relationships can begin to be established.

The opportunity to experience meaningful social communication, appropriate to their peer group, is not always readily available. Therefore, the opportunity to develop their social skills is limited and they are dependent on others (usually adults) to interpret their responses and needs. The opportunity to be included within mainstream environments facilitates the development of social skills for these children.

Poor body image

Many children with multiple disabilities are unaware of the parts of their own body and are unable to relate them to the body as a whole. These children may not be aware that the head is at the top of the body and the toes are at its furthest point; they may not be aware that the things on the ends of their arms are called 'hands' and that they are connected to their arms and trunk.

These children may have a very distorted view of themselves with little spatial awareness of the environment. The greater the spatial area the more they get lost within it. Inability to control their own movements and the environment leads to confusion, and the inability to determine directionality (forwards and backwards) and laterality (left and right) makes learning a difficult and complex task.

Poor self-esteem

Some experience failure for most of the time due to their inability to perform tasks and to communicate with others, leading to a lack of choice and opportunity, and reliance on others to provide for their needs. Many are deprived of the most basic intrinsic motivation. Therefore, it is not surprising that they have poor self-image or self-esteem. It is very difficult to be positive about oneself with these difficulties.

When we experience failure we feel depressed and negative about ourselves. What often raises our self-esteem is success. Success and being able to do tasks makes us feel good about who and what we are. It inspires and motivates us to go on. Success breeds success. Failure breeds failure. The more we are able to give control back to these children, to help them make decisions and real choices, to help them to be independent and to encourage them in all their efforts, the more we are likely to bring about success. Being passive participants in the process of interaction creates apathy, low motivation and poor self-esteem. Incorporating an interactive approach and allowing children to be actively involved in activities improves their self-worth and their perception of themselves. It may be quicker to do the tasks for them, but we are often unaware that they are being disempowered in the process.

Poor sensory skills

Some children with multiple disabilities have effectively 'pulled down the shutters' and are not attending, or may have an aversion to, sensory information. They may have been over-stimulated and have shut down because they were unable to cope with the bombardment of sensory information. Maybe they have been under-stimulated and have failed to register sensation within their body processes.

Some children may be sensory-defensive and show extreme aversion to specific kinds of sensory information (e.g. slimy textures and sounds). This may be overcome by the adult's use of language and careful selection of sensory information presented to the child, allowing him to be able to organize his sensations within his body processes.

Poor speech and language

Many children with multiple disabilities do not use any speech at all. Some fail to speak coherently; others are only able to make requests on a simple level, related to their basic needs. Some stutter or do not speak clearly. Most are unable to think in abstract language terms and are lost if discussion is not related to concrete experience and the present.

Poor cognitive skills

Often children are forced to develop unique learning styles to compensate for their multiple disabilities. They lack the ability to anticipate future events or the results of their actions. They have memory difficulties and are unable to grasp concepts quickly and without much reinforcement. Their concentration span is often short and attention levels can be erratic and variable.

Problems related to medication

The effects of medication are an important variable in the learning process. Many children with disabilities receive a cocktail of medication – some to improve their medical condition, some medicines to counteract the effects of others. However, this cocktail does affect performance. Therefore, when planning activities we need to be aware of the effects of medicines and consider the most appropriate times for learning – when children are most alert and motivated (arousal periods). Some medicines will induce tiredness, vagueness and an inability to concentrate, leading to serious developmental lags. Awareness of the child's arousal times, when the child is not under the influence of medication, is crucial to effective teaching.

Eating problems

Eating is dependent upon the motor functioning and medical condition of the child. Some will take nourishment through gastronomy tubes (running from their nose to their stomach). Others may have a sensory defensiveness to food (e.g. an aversion to lumps in liquid) or they may have a reflux problem resulting in projectile vomiting.

All of us enjoy eating, or we should if we don't. This should also be true for all children with multiple disabilities. When considering the establishment of a nourishment programme, take account of the following:

● physical management
● environment
● timing and routines
● nutrition
● safety of the child and the adult helping the child to eat (feeder)
● choice of food
● equipment
● feeder (where the feeder should sit/stand and who replaces her when she is ill)
● team work and collaboration
● training

An assessment should be taken by a team of staff (including a physiotherapist, occupational therapist, speech therapist, parents and school staff). Other professionals such as the dietician and school nurse should provide input if necessary. The advice of the dietician may be required because of concerns about weight loss or obesity, supplements or tube feeding.

The eating environment needs to be happy, relaxed, safe and conducive to good practice and communication. Children should be with peers who can model appropriate eating behaviour and in environments reflective of their mainstream peer group.

Lunchtime should be an interactive and social experience and not rushed. Children should be allowed quality time to eat and communicate with others, including their support worker. However, it is sometimes necessary for the support worker to help the child to eat as quickly as possible in order to be free to help other children, and then to take him to the toilet so he can be ready for the afternoon session. Lunchtime may then become the most stressful time of the day rather than a relaxing and enjoyable experience.

Use mealtimes as opportunities for social communication, for expression of preferences or rejection, to reinforce 'Yes' and 'No' responses, and times of fun and enjoyment.

Good positioning is the foundation for improving eating and drinking skills. When sitting, feet, knees and hips to be at a right angle, bottom well back, shoulders are down, back slightly leaning forward, with good support and table at appropriate height and distance.

Equipment is important for encouraging independence, even if eating takes a little longer. Non-slip plate mats (dycem), rimmed plates/bowls, and angled spoons, knives and forks are all useful pieces of equipment. Correct seating and the use of prompts are part of a supportive environment for independent eating.

Liquidizing foods together is not a particularly effective approach to helping children to develop recognition of individual textures and tastes or to enhancing their enjoyment of eating. We wouldn't like all our food to be mixed together, so why should the child? If food has to be liquidized, different items can be individually blended and given to the children along with the appropriate language and interpretation. This may take more time to prepare but it is definitely worth it.

Staff will need training in the care of gastrostomy tubes, lifting and handling, basic hygiene and eating techniques.

An excellent guide to helping children to eat and drink independently is April Winstock's book, *The Practical Management of Eating and Drinking Difficulties in Children* (1994).

Other problems

Visual problems

Sometimes professionals can be preoccupied with physical and medical problems and place less stress on the importance of vision in learning. A lack of opportunity to develop visual skills (e.g. through visual stimulation) reduces the child's motivation to learn and understand the visual world around him. Vision empowers a child to have a greater awareness and knowledge of 'what is out there'; without it, perceptual difficulties can develop and the child may be unable to coordinate body and limb movements.

Hearing problems

The selection of auditory information leads to greater awareness and understanding of the world. Often we are able to habituate sounds (i.e. we block out unnecessary sounds and attend only to those required). We often block out a clock ticking and 'white' noises, while attending to a speaker. Many children with multiple disabilities are unable to do this and need help. If help is not received they fail to attend to auditory information and this sensory channel becomes less meaningful and useful to them.

Unacceptable behaviours

Many children will perform behaviours that are not readily accepted as normal behavioural patterns. These may include rocking, eye poking, twirling, light gazing, hand-flapping and head-banging, to mention just a few. The reasons for these behaviours are not always easy to identify but many of these behaviours are exhibited in order to self-stimulate. Providing an equally rewarding activity often reduces and changes these patterns of behaviour. Providing appropriate role models also facilitates changes.

Fatigue

Finally, because of their disabilities, children have to work much harder to achieve tasks and gain success and control. Therefore, it is not surprising that they can quite quickly become tired and suffer from fatigue. We need to make sure that we are aware of children's arousal levels, and that we offer learning opportunities at appropriate times. Short bursts of learning followed by rest periods may be the best approach.

Implications for multiple-disabled children

Slower progress

The more multiple disabled and complex the child is, the slower progress is likely to be. In contrast, the mainstream child tends to learn progressively and quickly.

Regression

Progress can be disrupted by problems with feeding, sleeping, illness and a host of medical reasons. Often a relapse in a child's physical condition, or even a bad night, can set back progress.

Coordinating support

The greater number of disabilities the child has, the more people there are involved. The more people involved, the more agencies are involved. The greater the number of agencies, the more difficult it becomes to coordinate them and to understand their language codes. Each agency speaks with their own jargon and language. The physiotherapist will speak one way, the occupational therapist another, and so on.

More anomalies and problems

Additional problems create more anomalies. The ways in which these anomalies are interpreted to understand and support the child often produces further difficulties. The greater the permutation of difficulty, the more complex the needs of the child become. As the needs of the child become more complex, so there are fewer specialists available to work with him.

Higher level of staffing support and resources

Many children require a high level of support for their nursing/medical needs and for physical care. They will often need one-to-one help with feeding, toileting, dressing and most basic self-help tasks. The need for good postural seating is essential for teaching. Children will require environmental adaptations and specialist equipment and learning materials.

Changes to teaching and the curriculum

Adaptations to assessment procedures, teaching methods, communication approaches and the curriculum will be required if children are to succeed.

Common conditions

There are numerous conditions associated with children who are multiple disabled. Some children will exhibit more than one of the conditions below. It is important, however, that professionals and relevant people understand the nature and implications (aetiology) of conditions so that they can apply this knowledge in a classroom situation.

Asthma

This is a condition where there is a reversible narrowing of the airways in the lung due to inflammation, which causes swelling of the lining and spasm of the muscle around the airway. It may be caused by allergic reaction to inhaled, ingested or injected substances. Viral infections, exercise and smoke can also cause attacks. Children become wheezy and inhaled medication is often required. In severe cases the condition can be life-threatening.

Cerebral visual impairment (cortical blindness)

This is where the orbit or eye is not damaged but the optic nerve, pathway and tracts to the visual cortex are damaged. Children with this condition see and process visual information in a very distorted way and require a lot of help in interpreting what they see.

Cerebral auditory impairment

This is where the outer and middle ear are not damaged, but the auditory nerve, pathway and tracts to the auditory cortex are damaged. Children with this condition have a hearing impairment and process auditory information in a distorted way, requiring a lot of help in interpreting what they hear. This condition is not always readily supported by support services.

Cerebral palsy

This is not a disease, but a condition caused by the dysfunction of the cerebral cortex (the brain), usually the result of infection during pregnancy (i.e. rubella) or after birth (e.g. meningitis, encephalitis). It affects motor development and many have difficulty with head control, body posture and balance. Often these children have visual difficulties in the short or long term. The support group for this condition is Scope (formerly the Spastics Society).

There are four main types of cerebral palsy: spastic, athetoid, ataxic and mixed. Spastic cerebral palsy is caused by damage to the cerebral cortex and the child will be stiff in one or more limbs and possibly all over (hypertonia). Athetoid cerebral palsy is caused by damage to the basal ganglia and children will be floppy in one or more limbs (hypotonia). Ataxic cerebral palsy is caused by damage to the cerebellum. Movement is random and involuntary and many of these children find motor control very difficult. Mixed cerebral palsy encompasses those children who do not fit in any of the above categories (hypotonic).

Cerebral palsy is most commonly classified topographically (in terms of the parts of the body affected) as follows: quadriplegia (all four limbs); diplegia (all four limbs, legs are more affected than arms); paraplegia (both legs affected); triplegia (three limbs affected); hemiplegia (one side of the body); and monoplegia (one limb affected).

Cleft palate/cleft lip

This exists where there is a depression in the lip or palate. In early pregnancy, separate areas of the face and head develop individually and then join together. This condition occurs when this fails to happen. Some children with cleft palate have speech difficulties, but with early intervention most of these difficulties can be overcome. This is treated later in life by surgery.

Cystic fibrosis

This is the commonest inherited life-threatening disorder. The average age of survival is around 30 years. The condition causes glands to produce abnormally thick mucus and excessive salt. It involves the lungs and the pancreas, and both these areas become filled with mucus. Diabetes is common in these cases. Tiredness and weakness is characteristic of these children.

Cytomegalovirus (CMV)

This is a common virus that passes unnoticed or may be exhibited in mild flu-like symptoms. If a woman catches CMV during her pregnancy, the virus may be passed on to the foetus. Damage may cause blindness, deafness, spasticity and developmental delay. The HIV virus is part of this group and babies infected often die within the first five years of life.

Diabetes

This is a condition in which the body does not produce enough insulin to enable the body to use the carbohydrate (starch and sugars) eaten. The usual treatment is to inject the correct amount of insulin to enable the body to use the carbohydrate effectively. An inbalance in the insulin level can cause erratic behaviour, a lack of concentration and emotional trauma.

Developmental delay

Children who have undiagnosed conditions but clearly have difficulties in learning are often referred to as having global developmental delay.

Dystonia

This is a term for a group of neurological disorders in which muscle spasms occur, leading to abnormal postures. It tends to be most evident when the person is walking.

Eczema

This is a non-contagious inflammatory disease of the skin with itching, redness and a burning sensation. The severity of itching leads to a rash.

Certain foods may aggravate eczema (e.g. milk, eggs and additives). External factors which may trigger eczema include fibres, soaps, detergents, dust, water, grass, pollen or severe temperatures (hot and cold).

Encephalitis

This is a congenital condition and is caused by viral or bacterial infections. It results in the inflammation of the brain. The symptoms vary according to the area of the brain affected. However, it can manifest itself in convulsions, muscular weakness, rapid eye movements, facial weakness and involuntary movements. This can be a life-threatening condition. Medication is often prescribed.

Epilepsy

The cause of epilepsy is a temporary change in the way brain cells work. Epilepsy is a tendency to have recurrent seizures or 'absences' originating in the brain as a result of excessive discharge of brain cells. This is both a congenital and genetic condition. Children who suffer from brain injury may also have this condition.

Seizures can be generalized (which can also be known as 'grand mal') and this is where consciousness can be lost. The seizures include major convulsions and jerking and stiffening of limbs. Partial seizures (known as 'petit mal') result in temporary absence or vagueness, and loss of consciousness does not occur.

Seizures can be triggered by:

● stress
● patterns of light for those who are photosensitive
● lack of sleep
● high temperature and
● poor diet and skipping meals.

How to deal with a seizure?

● Cushion the head with something soft.
● Do not give them anything to drink or put in the mouth.
● Loosen clothing around their neck.
● Lie them on the floor or put them in the recovery position.
● Keep calm and reassure the person.

- Provide a place of safety.
- If the seizure continues for more than five minutes call an ambulance.

Haemophilia (or Von Willeband Syndrome)

This is an inherited blood disorder characterized by a defect in the blood-clotting system. In this condition, easy bruising and internal bleeding are common. In some cases, bleeding into the joints is a problem and can lead to long-term joint damage. Treatment includes intravenous injection of the missing clotting factor. This condition leads to tiredness and weakness, and often children may be absent from school for patchy periods of time to recover.

Hemiplegia

This is a congenital condition and means weakness of one side of the body due to disease or damage to the cerebral cortex. It leads to weakness in motor function and may affect the whole brain or either side. It is quite a complicated condition and this complexity depends largely on the areas of the brain affected. Medical knowledge of the damaged areas is crucial in determining educational implications. These children may have memory and motor dysfunction problems with physical palsy.

Hydrocephalus (known as 'water on the brain')

This is a congenital condition and is associated with spina bifida, meningitis and toxoplasmosis. It manifests itself in a blockage and accumulation of watery fluid (known as cerebro-spinal fluid) flowing through narrow pathways over the inside of the brain and down the spinal cord. This is remedied by a shunt or valve fitted to the back of the head which redirects this fluid. Shunts can become blocked, leading to headaches, nausea and photophobia. Shunts should be checked regularly and are often replaced every two or three years.

Infantile convulsions

These are convulsions that occur in infancy resulting in a violent involuntary contraction or spasm of muscles. They are often triggered when a child has a temperature and are often treated in a similar way to epilepsy, but in one single treatment.

Meningitis

This is caused by viral or bacterial infection and results in an inflammation of the lining to the brain. Bacterial meningitis is caused by influenza, listeria and the E.Coli bacteria, and can be fatal. Viral meningitis is commonly caused by mumps. Complications of meningitis include deafness, brain damage, epilepsy and visual impairment.

Microcephaly

As the name indicates, this is a defect in the growth of the brain, resulting in a smaller than normal growth. It can be inherited or congenital, and is prevalent in children with rubella, cytomegalovirus (CMV) and those with syndromes. It affects motor and visual development.

Mucopolysaccharide diseases

These are life-threatening and are a result of an inheritable genetic metabolic disorder. They cause errors in the body's metabolism where chemicals or enzymes are absent, leading to overdose of one or more of the chemicals which are essential for life. The body slowly destroys itself. This is linked to a number of syndromes, which include Hurler, Hunter, Sanfilippo and Battens. All are related to visual impairment and sensory dysfunction. There is little treatment available for these diseases. Bone marrow transplant may be considered, or gene therapy and enzyme replacement therapy.

Multiple sclerosis

This is a neurological condition caused by damage to the central nervous system as a result of the thinning of the coating around the nerve (myelin sheath) and produces scarring (sclerosis). With this condition, the nerve fibres stop conducting messages. This leads to balance difficulties, muscular spasms, tingling, visual impairment and double vision, loss of coordination, clumsiness, slurred speech, incontinence, fatigue and dizziness. Older children are mainly affected.

Muscular dystrophy

This affects several thousand children in the UK. It is a progressive degenerative, inherited neuromuscular disorder affecting the face, hands and respiratory system. The condition affects the motor nerve cells in the brain stem and spinal cord, and the nerve cells in the muscle fibres. It leads to muscular weakness, and often splints, braces, surgical corsets or wheelchairs are required to help these children.

Niemann-Pick disease

This disease is a progressive neurological condition that is caused by an accumulation of fats in the liver, spleen and bone marrow. This is life threatening, and rapid deterioration often follows, including dystonia, perceptual difficulties, and speech and visual impairment.

Osteogenesis imperfectica (known as 'brittle bones')

This is an inherited group of conditions caused by a fault in the protein structure of the bone, mainly a calcium or collagen deficiency. It manifests itself in a tendency to fracture or break bones easily. This condition improves with age; however, the later years may show postural deformities. These children are often 'dwarfed' with shortened or humped backs. A bone marrow transplant is sometimes performed to improve this condition. Life expectancy is often uncertain, and visual impairment is usually present due to optic nerve compression. Osteoporosis is part of this group and is characterized by reduced bone density.

Rhesus incompatibility

Some people's blood contains a substance called the Rhesus factor. When this is present, it is known as Rhesus positive blood. If blood does not contain this factor it is known as Rhesus negative.

Problems occur when the mother and child's Rhesus blood factor is different. When this happens, the mother's blood becomes infected, as the Rhesus factor is considered poisonous. The body reacts by producing antibodies. The consequence is that during the first pregnancy, the concentration of antibodies remains low. However, in subsequent pregnancies the antibody concentration can destroy the baby's red blood cells and release a substance known as bilirubin into the child's bloodstream. As a result, a child may be born with a sensory-neural hearing loss. All mothers are now tested for the Rhesus factor during their first pregnancy and if it is present they are given an injection immediately after the first baby is born.

Rheumatoid arthritis (Stills disease)

This affects some children, resulting in the inflammation of joints and arthritis. The symptoms include pain and difficulty in moving. Often steroids are used to thicken the cartilage in the joints. Tiredness, fatigue and pain are characteristic of this condition.

Rubella

The predominant cause of congenital deafblindness used to be rubella, commonly called German measles. Though this is normally a mild disease, infection during pregnancy, especially in the early stages of foetal development, can affect the baby.

Vaccination has reduced this condition; however, the failure of mothers to be vaccinated or to receive a booster vaccination has led to a resurgence of cases.

Deafblindness may also be aquired as a result of infection after birth, such as meningitis. Some causes of deafblindness such as Usher Syndrome are inherited.

Deafblind children have a combination of visual and hearing loss, which creates a unique pattern of learning difficulties. Many will require adapted or augmented forms of communication and will experience difficulties in the development of movement and mobility skills. They will experience difficulties integrating the information received from their other senses.

Sickle cell

This is an inheritable genetic disorder in which there is an abnormality of the haemoglobin which carries oxygen to the various organs of the body. The sickle shape of the haemoglobin causes cells to clump together, making their passage through arteries and veins very difficult. It causes pains in the joints and abdomen, dehydration, weakness and tiredness. It can be life threatening, resulting in seizures and strokes. This is a more common condition amongst people of African and Caribbean origin.

Traumatic brain damage

This can be caused by accidents or extreme stress or emotional upset, resulting in forms of cerebral palsy.

Toxoplasmosis

This is an infection caused by a parasite contained within raw or under-cooked meat, and food contaminated with infected cat faeces. This infection is easily transmitted to the foetus. Damage includes hydrocephalus, epilepsy, developmental delay and damage to the retina.

Syndromes

All syndromes are genetic and can be life threatening. A syndrome is a group of symptoms or features occurring together, often enough to constitute a disorder to which a name is given.

CHARGE

This is a rare syndrome and is an acronym for **C**oloboma (visual impairment); **H**eart Defect; **A**tresia of choanae (blockage of nasal passage); **R**etarded growth; **G**enital hypoplasia (undescended testicles, small penis); and **E**ar anomalies (hearing impairment and absence of the semi-circular canals).

The causes of CHARGE are not yet known. There is a wide variation between individuals with CHARGE and not all those with this condition are affected in every element. There are also many anomalies including abnormal gait, facial palsy, hypotonia, scoliosis and hypocalcaemia.

Down's Syndrome

This is a chromosomal disorder which occurs when, instead of the normal complement of two copies of chromosome 21, there is an additional chromosome. Most cases of Down's Syndrome are sporadic but there is a small risk of recurrence in further pregnancies within the same family. It is generally considered that the older the mother is, the greater the risk is that she will have a child with Down's Syndrome. However, statistically, most children who are Down's Syndrome who are born today are from younger mothers.

Those with Down's Syndrome have striking physical characteristics including thick fingers and toes, pear-shaped abdomen, dwarf appearance and obesity. They may suffer from myopia, balance and coordination difficulties, speech difficulties and mild to moderate hearing loss. All have moderate to severe learning difficulties.

Lawrence-Moon Biedl

This condition is a result of four chromosome defects. Children with this condition often have severe learning difficulties and may have additional fingers and toes. They are usually physically mature for their age, are obese and have a delay in processing information. They may have a severe visual impairment, which may include retinal dystrophy or retinitis pigmentosa.

A sub-group of the condition is Bardet Biedl, which is similar, but results in mild to moderate learning difficulties.

Lebers Amaurosis

This condition is a result of gene deficiency. It causes blindness or severe visual impairment from birth. Some children may have retinal dystrophy, retinitis pigmentosa or only have light perception.

Marfans

This is caused by a mutation in the gene fibrillin located in chromosome 15. This protein deficiency leads to weakness of the joints and limbs, and a heart defect. Sufferers often have visual impairment (e.g. dislocation of the lenses). They have skeletal scoliosis (curvature of the spine). They are usually tall and slim, with long fingers and a pointed nose. Intelligence is not affected.

Usher

This is a genetic condition characterized by sensory neural hearing loss with severe visual impairment. The hearing loss is congenital and may be total or partial. The visual impairment comes in the form of retinitis pigmentosa, which is a progressive deterioration of the retina that causes night blindness, tunnel vision and severe central visual loss. Poor balance is also a problem.

There are three types of the syndrome. Type I is characterized by profound hearing loss, poor balance and retinitis pigmentosa, before the age of ten. Type II presents moderate to severe hearing loss, normal balance and retinitis pigmentosa, developing in the late teens. Type III is characterized by progressive hearing and visual loss, generally with onset around 20 to 30 years of age.

Specific problems for parents

Overcoming guilt

This is often the first major problem facing parents, especially if the disease has been inherited or is congenital. The phrase 'It's all my fault' is heard time and time again. The more the parents blame themselves the more guilty they feel. For some, the shock of knowing the consequences of bringing into the world a child who is disabled brings heartbreak, numbness, depression, anger, tears and disbelief. For many, guilt comes in stages. Coping with how to help the child, finding out what he will need and who will need to be involved initially occupies their minds and redirects their thoughts. This delays or interrupts their feelings of guilt. But for many, the period of overcoming guilt is long and drawn out and the process is both painful and exacting. Guilt brings self doubt and a lowering of self-esteem.

Adjusting to another disability

With children who have many complex needs, parents need to keep adjusting to being told about another disability or problem that their child has. When this happens, it is often difficult to take a positive view of the child's learning potential and future progress. Parents have to accept another disability, another problem and another thing to be guilty about. Another disability often means additional equipment (e.g. hearing aids, spectacles).

Many problems mean many specialists

Some parents may come into contact with as many as 20 professionals who are involved with helping their child. The timetabling of appointments and adjusting to the wide range of different vocabulary used by all these professionals is challenging and hard work. Often the child can be treated as a collection of bits, whereas a holistic view that considers the child's needs as a whole is really what is needed. If this is not carefully monitored and coordinated then it can be very confusing and non-productive to the parents, professionals and the child. The task of coordinating these professionals often has to be done by the parents.

Difficulties with being a family

Many parents feel that it is difficult to share family activities with their child. Some feel embarrassed or ashamed, but activities do exist that enable all to be involved as a family. This is just a short list of possibilities: walking, shopping, listening to music, going to the cinema, aerobics, trampolining, riding a tandem bicycle or tricycle, ten-pin bowling, swimming, canoeing and sailing. Society will accept and adapt if it is given the opportunity and experience of meeting children of all disabilities.

For some families, the social life of its members can be curtailed or reduced. The provision of care often disrupts family relationships and can lead to resentment and jealosy. As time, energy and resources are given to the child with multiple disabilities, other children will always take second, third or fourth place. The element of fun, enjoyment and relaxation can be missing unless the parents work hard to incorporate this into the routine life of the family. The opportunity of having a holiday (especially abroad) becomes akin to a planning assault course with so many obstacles to plan and overcome.

Finding the right professional

Much encouragement and relief comes when professionals are able to understand the nature of a parent's problems, recognize the capabilities of the child and show a positive, knowledgeable and empathetic approach to the range of difficulties encountered.

Scarcity of expertise

The more complex the needs of the child, and the lower the incidence of his particular problems, the more difficult it becomes to find the right professionals to help. Also it is more difficult to place the child in existing provision that may not be tailor-made.

Bureaucracy

Parents may encounter frustration and bewilderment with bureaucracy at all levels. They may experience extreme stress through having to complete large numbers of forms and having to travel to a number of locations. Many parents may have contacts with the health service through the hospitals, child development clinics and therapy services. Social services are consulted for home modifications and social support, and education services are needed for pre-school and school provision.

Access to services

Knowledge of the services available is always a difficult task. Despite the number of referrals that are made by social work teams, access and availability in the public and voluntary sectors is not always clear and forthcoming.

Parents feel supported by rapid referral processes and by being respected and listened to. Being told exactly what is happening is very important and allays fears. However, access to services tends to be a long, winding road that can seem endless to parents. The system may be impersonal and not always sympathetic to their needs and pressures.

Marital strain

Having a child with multiple disabilities can either pull a marriage apart or can bring the couple closer together. However, the number of single parents with these children is increasing.

The centre of conversation often moves away from them and their relationship together towards the child. The lack of quality time alone together and the freedom to go out regularly is often reduced. Couples can drift away from each other but might feel obliged to stay together for their children's sake. Having a strong support network (such as family or friends) to give the couple and family 'time out' is essential. Respite care from public/voluntary services also becomes a lifeline.

Family support

The acceptance of this child into the family is vitally important. A child born into an extended family, who regularly sees grandparents, aunts and uncles, will benefit significantly from this contact. However, different networks may emerge in their place through friendships and community groups when a close family system is missing. Some parents may try to conceal the truth and hide their child from society, even though that community and culture would embrace and fully accept the child and his disabilities. Parents may find it difficult to mix or seek help from other families if their child is disabled. They may feel embarrased and guilty when they are around others or be too proud to accept the help of voluntary groups (i.e. religious organizations, youth clubs, parent support groups and respite care agencies). Other families may embrace the support of others and of their community.

Adapting the home

The more multiple disabled the child is, the more likely it is that the home will need to be adapted to incorporate hoists, stairlifts, stair rails, respirators and adjustable furniture. The parents will need to

26

work hard at keeping the home as a home, rather than a hospital. A hoist could be in the lounge, bathroom and bedroom and the atmosphere of the home can easily be changed if it is not monitored or deliberately checked.

Financial restraints

Respite care, building adaptations, equipment, resources, dietary requirements and child-minding facilities all incur a financial burden on the family. Although financial support may be given by grants or council, the bureacracy and negotiations required are usually time consuming and stressful. Often money is raised by the couple themselves, family and friends, charities or gifts.

Future

The future care of the child is one of major concern. Anxiety is caused by two isues: the parents' inability to care for their children due to old age or sickness and what will happen to the child after their death. Often these issues are sidelined and each day is treated separately: 'Let's take one day at a time'. Parents often make provision for these events, but it does not always match the standard of care they would like or expect. Sometimes, the responsibility may fall to siblings, although this is rare. However, the continuity of support will undoubtedly continue through the sibling route out of love to their brother or sister.

Diet and Behaviour

'Food that is good for the heart is likely to be good for the brain.'
Hippocrates (450BC)

Hippocrates was right all those years ago, food does affect our health and impact upon our development, growth and behaviour. It is true that certain types of food increase our concentration and improve the function of the brain. Diet has particularly been helpful in reducing ADHD, dyslexia, dyspraxia, neurodevelopmental anomalies, sleep and mood disorders. The secret lies in the dependency of the brain and its neurolgical development upon long-chain polyunsaturated fatty acids (LCPs). LCPs are the building blocks for growth and maintenance of nerve cells within the brain. The body is unable to produce LCPs and relies on food intake to provide this need. Low intake of LCPs leads to deficiencies. LCPs are located in all foods, however, some contain a high inbalance level of omega 3 and 6. The foods with the correct ratio are the ones that identify the appropriate LCP level. The appropriate ratio is 2:1 to 10:1 in favour of omega 6.

Fish are the richest sources of omega 3, mackerel and pilchards being the highest. Meat provides the highest source of omega 6, (beef being the highest). Cooking oil is also important, the best ones being canola, olive and soybean. Avoid cheap oils and vegetable oil.

2

Fruit is a good source of vitamin A, B and C. Dried fruit is particular high in fibre, iron, potassium and selenium. Apricots help growth and healthy hair, skin, teeth and eyes. They are high in magnesium and calcium and help prevent osteoporosis. Bananas are low in fat and high in energy. They have a high content of iron, potassium, fibre and vitamin B and they help to prevent anaemia, high blood pressure and depression.

High levels of salt and sugar are believed to trigger hyperactivity and are also linked with increased tinnitus. Avoiding crisps, sweets and soft drinks has proven beneficial, as has a low-salt diet.

Nuts and seeds are also good food sources, however, they are not low in fat. Walnuts keep cholesterol levels healthy and contain melatoin which may help sleep–wake cycles. Almonds are cholesterol-free and help maintain a healthy heart. Prunes maintain bowel regularity and figs help the digestive system. Brazil nuts ensure a healthy immune system and thyroid function.

Zinc deficiency affects neurological growth and breaks down tissues. Red meat and some seafoods are the best dietary sources. Many ADHD children have magnesium deficiency. Magnesium is important for muscle and nerve function. Food rich in magnesium include nuts, cereals and green leafy vegetables. Food supplements are alternatives to natural products. A good guide to this subject is Stordy (2000), or go to any good health food shop.

Key points

- There is a wide range of possible difficulties and problems that a person who is multiple disabled may have. Awareness of these difficulties and applying this knowledge to teaching is essential to facilitate good practice.
- Slow progress and regression are often associated with this group of children, so don't be discouraged!
- The more disabilities the child has, the more professionals are likely to be involved.
- Additional problems create more anomalies.
- Find out as much information as possible about the child and their associated conditions. Use this information to guide interactions and learning.
- Knowledge and understanding of the nature of the child's medical condition is important to guide learning.
- Parents need help and support on a number of issues; these may include overcoming guilt, adjusting to the child's other disabilities, coordinating professionals, finding the right professional with the appropriate expertise, handling bureaucracy and family support.

3 | Developing effective communication skills

Sarah is eight years old and is deafblind. She has a little light perception in both eyes. Eighteen months ago she was identified as having a moderate to severe sensori-neural hearing loss and she wears post-aural hearing aids in both ears. She was recently diagnosed as having diabetes and as a result has insulin injections every day and her blood tested three times a day. She is educated in a mainstream school in accordance with her parents' wishes and receives full-time support. In the last two years, she has learned to speak and will state her preferences and answer questions appropriately. She is learning to use a Perkins Brailler and is beginning to identify words in Braille. Sarah is learning to finger-spell three-lettered words using the deafblind alphabet. She is learning to link phonic skills to words and knows many of the sounds of the alphabet. To aid her understanding of speech she sometimes uses a modified version of the Tadoma method. Sarah loves singing and this has proven an effective way of unlocking the door into her world to channel learning. Sarah is learning to use a long cane for indoor and outdoor mobility.

'Communication can be summed up as our attempts to obtain information from and impose order upon the world around us.'

McInnes and Treffry (1984)

Communication is vitally important. It gives us power to control our lives and links us to the world around us. Communication can be very basic and it can also be very complicated, ranging from changes in body movements and vocalization to using objects, symbols or signs and speech. All are important and a variety of communication systems may need to be used as the child develops. The child may choose one or prefer a combination of communication modes.

Communication takes place all the time and is an integral part of the process of learning. Communication cannot be put into a timetable slot. It takes place inside and outside the classroom, in the toilet and dining room, at home and at school. Communication is the ability to 'get the message across': the ability of the initiator to convey a message and the recipient to understand messages being sent and to respond by conveying his own needs: it is a key part of life.

Communication is a key part of a child's ability to interact with and control his immediate environment. For many children with multiple disabilities this is very difficult. Their entire world is locked within their own body. Unlocking the door to their world is the challenge that we face. As Van Dijk (1966) stated:

'We soon discovered that these children are so bound up in their own world that they make no contacts and no relationships. Some do not know themselves. We cannot put such a child on a chair in a classroom putting pegs in holes or

shapes in a form board. We must start where the child is. That is still within his own body. We have to develop his ego-consciousness so that he knows "I am. This is me."'

At birth, and in the early years of life, it is almost impossible to assess the level of impairment accurately in all developmental areas. The baby's health may be generally good. The baby will feed normally, smile occasionally, move his legs and arms and seem content. The first noticeable sign that something is wrong is that the baby is passive. There is a lack of eye contact. The smile is seen less often, the random movement of the limbs declines. After initially sleeping well, the baby becomes restless and demands a great deal of physical contact. Learning and development are taking place, but without the means to communicate with his mother through the natural and visual route. The most effective means of communication and gaining physical contact will be through screaming or crying. The baby's attempts to explore the world are lost in the void of space. If objects are not within close eye range, then they are either not seen at all or are lost within the baby's environment. This often leads to frustration, fear and withdrawal from the world. It is therefore much harder for him to interpret what is happening in his immediate surrounds.

Many children with multiple disabilities will habitually startle when touched or lifted if they are not given consistent and appropriate warnings of forthcoming events (for example, nappy-changing, bath time or being picked up). All of these experiences should be fun, confidence-building and sociable events, but they can become frightening and confusing. Even if they are able to cope with everyday events, these children will need a lot of help to interpret sound in their environment (e.g. everyday sounds of the washing machine, radio, door shutting, vacuum cleaner) and more importantly, speech and conversation.

The child's own sounds need to be given meaning. In normal development, a child learns this naturally and slowly. The child will not always react to his parent's voice shouted from another room. It is only when the adult moves closer to the child that the child is able to connect the person and the voice.

For these children, there are difficulties in developing early interactive skills. From an early age, mutual gaze and visual exchange help in the formation of an emotional bond. Later, a baby will direct his mother's attention by eye-pointing. This ability to direct the adult's attention is an important early skill. Later, more formalized pre-verbal skills develop (e.g. gesturing, pointing and turning towards or away from an object), and these, again, are often absent from the repertoire of the multiple-disabled child.

Children with very complex needs are particularly at risk during early infancy. Without the appropriate support they may give up and become passive, and they will be unaware of the extent to which they can enjoy interactive exchanges or refer to and obtain objects and activities.

Children with multiple disabilities often have a wide repertoire of facial expressions which provide information to which parents and other adults can respond. These children are often not good initiators and can become very passive, particularly in movement and mobility. It is often necessary for the adult to wait a long time, with long gaps in the interaction, to show the child that if he wants an action to happen again, he has got to do something to make it happen. Many adults feel that if nothing is happening, they have to make it happen by doing something. This can lead the adult to dominate the interaction and activities. The child may well respond with pleasure, but he is not in charge of the interaction.

These children need to be carefully observed in order for the adult to pick up on those movements that are intentional. This is not always easy when the child's movement pattern may be erratic and uncoordinated. When his movements have been established as pleasurable and motivating, then the adult can begin to interpret them more deliberately and be able to understand the child's requests.

The signals that babies use to communicate include: body movements and gestures; crying; eye-contact; avoidance and turning away; vocalizing speech-like sounds; sleeping; pushing away; throwing objects; smiling; vomiting; hitting; pulling hair; biting; scratching; changes in breathing patterns; mouthing; eye-pointing; spitting; and hand-stroking. Babies communicate for a number of reasons. They need to express their needs (discomfort, pain, hunger, temperature, fear), and to get attention (I'm the most important person). They want to explore their environment. They are curious and seek lots of rewards and they wish to be in control and manipulate situations. Communication provides the means to these ends.

Children need to communicate four basic wants. These are 'yes', 'no', 'more of' and 'less of'. It is crucial that the individual working with the child is able to cue into the child's interaction and be intuitive to his communication mode. Adult and child will need to develop a close bond or rapport similar to the early bonding of the mother and her child if this intuition is to be present. It may be necessary to ask significant adults (e.g. parents, teachers) who regularly work with the child to assist you in determining these communication exchanges. It is necessary throughout the exchange to keep asking the child if he wants more and not to continue the activity unless a response is elicited, so that the child feels in control.

Role of an Intervenor or Intensive Interaction

An intervenor approach is also referred to as 'intensive interaction'. Intensive Interaction was developed during the 1980s by staff at Harperbury Hospital School, Hertfordshire, England. Hewett and Nind (1998), who were teachers at the school, described the approach as intervention based on the model established by mother and child interaction, where mother and child engage in simple turn-taking, the mother responding to what the baby does by imitation and following a cause and effect to communication. They also describe the interactions as intensive, mutually enjoyable interactive games that makes learning easier and playful. The term 'Intervenor' has been widely introduced by McInnes and Treffry (1984) and Nielsen (1992). In this book I will draw together all these views and methods under the term 'Intervenor'.

An Intervenor provides the link between our world and the world of the child. It is by us entering their world and interacting in their conceptual understanding that we can introduce and bring them into our world. In the same way, if we visit a foreign country, we attempt to interface with its culture. If we don't, we miss out on its ingredients and variety. But by embracing its culture and relating it to our own, we can enjoy its richness and beauty.

Many multiple-disabled children live in a world of their own, which is egocentric, self-stimulating and motivating. If our world is confusing, unstimulating and unexciting, then they will shut down and enter their own world that offers more. The challenge that faces the Intervenor (you and me) is the ability to interface and break into their world and offer something different. Acknowledge their intricacies and their 'Yes' and 'No' responses, if they be gestural (e.g. breathing patterns and body movements), as well as verbal cues (intonation and volume pattern). In this way we can respect and value them for who they are, and help the child to gain control over his life and to influence the world.

Lee and MacWilliam (2005) identified four principles to keep in mind with interventions. The first is to 'tune in', which simply means to react to what the child is offering at that moment, building it into a communicative exchange. The second is watching. This involves acute observation skills, reading the child's signals and interpreting what the child is trying to convey. Next, it is important to wait and give the child plenty of time to respond. Finally, the child's responses need to be followed by adult responses using movement and sound.

Children with multiple disabilities may require the full-time support of an intervenor. Intervention is the process which allows the child to act on his environment. An intervenor is a person who provides intervention for this child and mediates between the child and his environment to enable him to communicate effectively and receive non-distorted information that has been sorted from the environment. An intervenor will take on the role of developing a close rapport with the child, similar to the bond formed between mother and child.

Bond (1993) identified a number of critical features that an intervenor needs to foster. These are set out below.

Establishing effective roles and relationships

It is important to develop a close bond between Intervenor and child. Within this interaction, the child needs to feel safe and secure and to be able to trust the Intervenor. Interactions will need to provide the child with opportunities to imitate and model desired social communication, and through this relationship the child will be able to control his environment and develop decision-making and assertiveness skills.

Responsiveness and reciprocal influence

The child will learn to be more responsive to learning contexts and adults will be more responsive to the learner's initiatives and will wait for him to respond. The Intervenor will provide opportunities to perform, initiate, respond and practise newly acquired skills, allowing sufficient time for the child to process information.

The concept of sharing tasks

Within these interactions, tasks will become mutually beneficial and both participants will develop a positive liking for each other. They will begin to develop positive social relationships and the intervenor will start to recognize the positive qualities of the child as a learner.

Communication

The Intervenor will provide communication that is predictable, consistent and reliable. She will be aware of the modes of communication used by the child and how these are balanced by the child to process and understand the world around him.

Turn-taking

Turn-taking is an important aspect of developing effective communication skills. Often this concept is seen much later in the child's social development. However, its beginnings are in very early interaction, partly through cause and effect. The child learns that if he listens and attends, it will bring about rewards. The Intervenor will help him to be aware of the starts, pauses and ends of conversations. He will develop an understanding of another person's body language and become more responsive to the Intervenor's interactions and will learn to anticipate responses. The Intervenor will acknowledge and reinforce acceptable responses and develop and modify initiatives in response to reactions by others. The child will learn to share his life with another, sharing skills, ideas and emotions.

Important Characteristics

1 The Intervenor should have a belief in herself that she is able to provide that link or connection with the child; the ability to turn the light on – to find the spark that will ignite the flame or match. Young children and peers often have this simple belief, because they see things more simply and value their friends for what they are. Adults make assumptions, see barriers and the disabilities

of the child. These assumptions influence their belief and faith in the child and this is all too apparent to the child in their first interaction. Therefore, it is important that the Intervenor's belief and faith in the child to communicate is evident to him in word, emotion and physical reaction. From this perspective, the child's individual mode of communication can be identified, respected and valued.

2 Interactions need to be carried out with intensity and sensitivity. This begins by getting to know the child within ritualized routines. Interactions then become more sophisticated and reciprocal and the child is enabled to take a more active role.

3 Throughout the interactions, the Intervenor modifies their interpersonal behaviours (i.e. facial expressions, body language, speech) to engage with the child. This may involve imitating speech or learner behaviour, matching rhythms of activity to the child and timing pauses and periods of activity. The Intervenor will watch carefully, wait, and will time their interactions.

4 The Intervenor responds to the child's behaviour and therefore creates an atmosphere of child-led activities. The Intervenor credits the child with thoughts, feelings and intentions and attributes meaning to actions and responds to these behaviours as if they had been said. The Intervenor tunes in closely to the child and begins to recognize reasons for certain behaviours which have been previously missed.

5 Music is a very powerful tool in the early interaction process of establishing contact. Using a 'Hello' song to introduce the session and yourself is particularly important with babies, young children and some older children.

6 Establishing a personal object of reference to represent yourself is also important. This provides a secure structure of consistency and enables the child to know who you are and what you represent. 'Here is Michael. I like Michael. He likes me. He understands me. What exciting things is Michael going to do with me today?' It will also help when you are away from the child. They will often remember this personal object for years. An example of this personal object of reference could be a wedding or engagement ring, bracelet or even a bristly chin. But remember that it must be readily available and can be replaced.

7 Physical contact and position are key elements in establishing an effective intervention and interaction. Before interaction takes place, a decision about the position of the Intervenor in relation to the child needs to be made. Ideally, placing the child on the floor will provide a position of closer intimacy and bond. The position you will adopt will depend upon on his mobility skills and ability to support himself. The photographs below illustrate a variety of positions that the Intervenor may use. It will be very clear what position the child favours by his early interaction with you. However, it is important that whatever position is favoured, that physical contact between Intervenor and child is maintained (i.e. your knees against his knees, your legs being wrapped around his body from behind or in front, your thighs against his thighs). This will provide a constant thermometer reading to you and the child, about how he is feeling and how he feels about you.

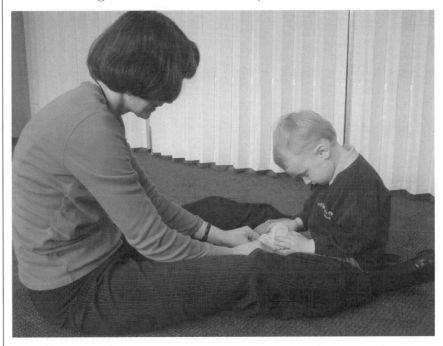

For example, during a plenary session or circle time on the carpet, being in front of the child will not be appropriate or possible. Therefore a position to the side or from behind will need to be maintained. This decision should be based on previous knowledge and inform from earlier interactions. The adult could either sit one side and a peer sit the other, with an additional arm prompt from the Intervenor.

The Intervenor could sit from behind, kneeling down with her chest and stomach against the back of the child.

Sitting from behind or to the side will also enable the Intervenor to whisper into the child's ear to provide additional support and commentary, without distracting other members of the class. This will help to fill in the language gaps and help the child to feel safe, more secure and less confused. Another position from behind the child is to wrap your legs around the child, with his back up against your chest. This would provide postural support and security to the child

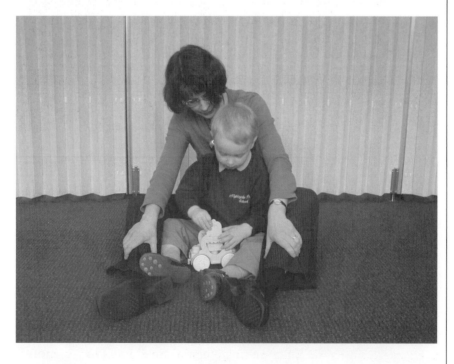

A buggy or push-along toy can also be used in an Intervenor-style approach by an adult and or peer, assisting in the activity.

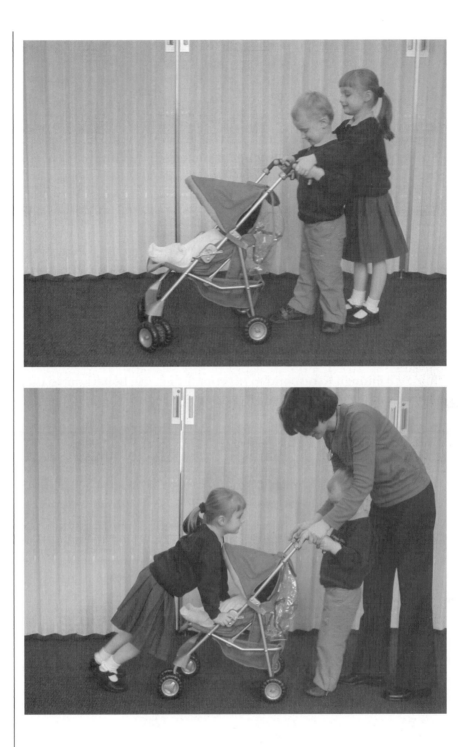

3

The physical contact aspect can be addressed in the school's policy.

8 Content is also important. Chose a selection of songs or activities to establish an effective bond and engage with the child. Plan before you interact and look out for the child's 'yes' and 'no' response.

9 'Do you want more?' is dependent on knowing the child's 'Yes' and 'No' responses. It is also dependent on providing pauses or stops when the question is asked and allowing sufficient time for them to respond. 'Shall we sing it again? Shall I talk to you more?' Wait for them to respond. Be patient and look for the cues. Maintaining a close physical contact and keeping to a consistent way of requesting 'More', will lead the Intervenor to reach the right decision about the child's communication skills.

In this way, the child learns to be part of the world, and we learn something of his conceptual understanding of the world he lives in. An effective intervenor is crucial in working with children with multiple disabilities. This bonding process cannot be underestimated. The intervenor needs to create a clear and structured environment alongside the teacher and other colleagues, and be a person who is available, consistent, responsive and as sensitive as possible. Many educationalists feel that the child should only have one person to support him, as this will reduce inconsistency, build up trust, and provide greater security to the child. However, this is not always a practical and realistic expectation, as that person may become ill or leave. It is therefore advisable that a limited number of Intervenors support the child (up to three), and that these people are interchanged consistently at appropriate times.

Part of the Intervenor's role will be to help others to understand the child well enough to respond to his communicative behaviour so that he, too, can become part of the social situation.

Identifying 'yes' and 'no'

Once contact has been made through the use of effective Intervenor skills, the next step is to ascertain the child's 'yes' and 'no' responses. All children have these, although the child may not be using them effectively or know how to use them because they have been ignored or not been valued. By engaging the child in pleasurable activity 'yes' and 'no' responses are identified and therefore become more meaningful to the child to control the outcomes of his world. Using an Intervenor approach, the identification of the 'yes' and 'no' response the process can be completed within 20 minutes or less.

The table below indicates possible 'yes' and 'no' responses that should be looked for when interacting with the child.

Yes	No
Smiling	Pushing away
Stilling	Agitated pitch pattern
Eye pointing	Biting
Eye contact	Scratching
Breathing pattern – fast/slow	Spitting
Bending head downwards/upwards	Shutting down
Intonation pattern – high or low pitch	Sleeping
Gurgling or babble	Breathing pattern – fast slow
Clapping	
Bending head downwards/upwards	Bending head downwards
Finger pointing	
Lifting arm or hand	Eye-blinking
Eye-blinking	

The child may use two or three 'yes' or 'no' cues, but these will be more apparent the more the Intervenor acknowledges these communication cues with the child and by affirming these cues with others who work with him. The 'no' response for one child may not be the same for another. All children are individuals and do not always conform to a set pattern. Discovering the correct cues presents an exciting challenge to the Intervenor and a liberating experience to the child.

All children have 'yes' or 'no' responses', we just don't know them. The challenge is to discover them. Using a video camera or an outside observer (parent, teaching assistant) will also help to affirm the decision.

Finding the Key

In the Introduction I stated that the need to find the key to unlock the door for learning is the challenge that faces us all. In the book *I raise my eyes to say* Yes, a hospital worker, Wessie, discovered this key while feeding Ruth, a severely disabled young girl, who was admitted to a residential institution and labelled an 'imbecile'.

'Wessie knew she was onto something, but she wasn't sure just what. She pondered for a few more seconds then it clicked! A silent conversation flashed between us as loud and clear as any spoken word. Even before she asked me a dozen times over, and before I exuberantly answered a dozen times with my eyes raised skyward, Wessie knew, and I knew that she knew, I was raising my eyes to say "Yes".'

The first key here was finding the 'yes' response and to link our world to her world. Then after this the key was to find the correct communication mode.

Selecting a communication mode

Before selecting an appropriate communication mode there are a number of underlying aspects to be considered.

● Professionals will need to look at the developmental level of the child and how he currently attempts to communicate. The nature of the child's vision and his multiple disabilities will need to be considered alongside the child's preferred method of communicating needs.

● The system should be child-centred and use appropriate vocabulary. It may be necessary to start with a short list of words and to gradually increase this list once the child has understood them and is ready to move on. Also, a balance needs to be struck between activities which may be infrequent but motivating to the child (e.g. swimming once a week) and others that are more frequent (e.g. meals, toilet, home time).

- It is essential that a team approach is used, but that a key person is identified to monitor, guide and coordinate its implementation. The approach needs to be fully embraced by all staff implementing it.

- Consistency and repetition are essential if the programme is to be successful. Without consistency the likelihood of success is minimal.

- Any changes within the communication system need to be introduced carefully, slowly and in small doses, then increased gradually.

- The communication system needs to move from concrete principles to abstract modes, from real to symbolic, from a small to large vocabulary, from simple to complex language structures. A communication system should be used in a concrete situation where the child is actively involved.

- It is important that speech is used to accompany all communication forms.

- Communication should have a clear structure. It should have a beginning and an end. In this way the child clearly begins to understand communication frameworks. The process of turn-taking can be built into the framework. Professionals need to concentrate on helping the child to express his needs, and allow him additional time to process replies.

- Communication needs to be exciting. Activities need to be reactive in their presentation and the adult needs to be reactive in her style, working within a framework of sensitivity and security.

Communication modes

If a person is unable to communicate using speech, then some other means of communication is required. This is often refered to as Augmentative or Alternative Communication (AAC). Those who use augmentative communication use it to supplement speech, whereas those who use alternative communication use it instead of speech. There is a wide variety of communication modes and these range from speech, writing, manual signs, natural gestures, pictures and line drawings, to symbols and objects of reference.

Speech

Encouraging children to use spoken words to convey meaning is, for most, the favoured system. However, many children with multiple disabilities are not able to vocalize words because of physical difficulties or lack of opportunities. Some professionals believe that if language and speech is presented sufficiently and consistently to children, then they will want to speak. Sometimes speech is not acquired by children with multiple disabilities because of a lack of self-belief. When working with children with multiple disabilities, clear, everyday language should be an essential element of all interaction. Single words and short sentences, spoken clearly, convey meaning more easily than complex sentences – shorter sentences make the organization of thought and sensory integration easier.

When using speech we are mainly using our visual and auditory pathways but speech can also use the tactile sense. The Tadoma method is a tactual way of reading the speech of others. To use this technique, the person places their hand on the speaker's face and neck. The thumb covers the speaker's mouth to feel the movements of the lips, jaw and tongue. The other four fingers are spread over the cheek, jaw and throat to detect vibrations.

Writing

This mode of communication focuses on the use of the visual and tactile senses. This route is often denied to, or is very difficult for children with multiple difficulties. However, words should always be written under pictures, line drawings or symbols in order to reinforce the spoken and written word. Children who are slow in writing or are unable to write may use many alternative methods at their disposal. These would include the use of tape recorders, voice recognition software, communication aids, computers and other access technology.

Manual signs

Manual signs focus on the use of the visual, auditory and tactile senses. Many signs will need to be adapted in different ways for different children, and formal signing systems may become unworkable. The mode of communication adopted will depend upon the needs and level of development of the child. If a formal system can be adopted, then the ability to communicate and share experiences with other users becomes possible within a framework of universal acceptance. However, if this is not possible, then we need to record an individual child's signs, so that all those involved with the child can understand his communication mode.

Signs should be introduced gradually and be integrated into a daily routine of activities: they can only be meaningful if they are related to the 'real thing'. Signs should always be accompanied by speech. No more than six signs should be introduced at the beginning. Useful signs include 'yes', 'no', 'wait', 'more', 'good' and 'finish'.

It is important to allow children more time to assimilate interactions and to respond to them. Often, we are too eager to move on to the next stage of interaction, before the child has had sufficient time to respond.

There are a number of manual signing systems:

British Sign Language (BSL)

This is the language used by people who are deaf from birth and consists of signs, finger spelling and natural gestures. BSL has its own grammatical structure which does not follow the English word order. It is a language in its own right.

Sign-supported English (SSE)

These are signs taken from BSL, together with finger spelling. It uses the English word order, to supplement spoken words on the lips.

Signed English (SE)

This is used to provide an exact grammatical signed representation of spoken English. Signed English is based on traditional signs and finger spelling with invented signs for the grammatical elements that are not present in traditional signing.

The Makaton vocabulary

This is a basic signing system which uses the key signs from BSL. It has a small and selective vocabulary of important words used in everyday life. This is a popular system and is widely used in schools today.

Signalong

Signalong is now widely used in education in England and is designed to help children and adults with multiple disabilities to acquire language and communication skills. It is a sign-supported system based on BSL, using sign in a spoken word order with one sign per concept. Signalong's extensive vocabulary (over 11,000 signs) can be used in all environments (home, school and community). It encourages eye contact and concentration, and needs no additional materials or equipment. Signs are interpreted according to handshape, orientation, placement and movement.

Cued speech

This system is based on speech, and is supported by hand shapes being made close to the mouth to enhance lip-reading skills. It is only used in a few schools now.

Hands-on or co-active signing

This is often used by people born deaf who have become blind. This is where the adult works alongside the child (either to the front or side or from behind) and guides him through the signs being introduced. Using this approach, the signs can become more concrete and meaningful to the child as his hands interact with the adult's. This approach has also been referred to by some professionals as 'body signing'.

It is important that the adult is careful not to manipulate the child's hands, as the child may be tactile-defensive and dislike having his hands touched, or he may need freedom to use his hands in order to gain information on the world around him. With this method, hands should be held lightly so that the child can use his hands freely if he wishes to do so.

Finger spelling

There are three different forms of finger spelling: the British Finger Spelling Alphabet; the Deafblind Manual Alphabet; and the Block Letter Alphabet. Finger spelling is especially useful for people's names and is often used in conjunction with another manual signing system.

Home-grown signs

Often children create their own signs, and when they do, these are substituted for other conventional signs. As adults we need to respect signs created by children and their chosen communication and accept their modifications, especially when it is physically difficult to produce the sign of a formal system. There is always a danger of formalizing a sign system for this particular target group as it can become less individualized, inflexible and not so child-centred.

Natural gestures

Natural gestures use mainly our visual, auditory and tactile senses. Some children might use hand and body movements to communicate meaning. A hand motion can be used to indicate 'yes' or 'no' and to make choices. Breathing patterns, facial expressions, vocalizations, grunts, sighs, eye-pointing and eye-blinking can be interpreted as other alternatives to natural gestures.

These gestures are very important to aid communication. A child's gestures will need to be documented, to help all those working with the child to understand what he is communicating.

Pictures or line drawings

The use of pictures is another communication mode. Initially, the pictures used are simple drawings of objects of reference; these gradually progress to more elaborate and complex representations, including black and white and coloured photographs. Links are established by colouring in pictures, matching objects to pictures and using raised and tactile diagrams.

Events and curriculum activities can be further explained by the Intervenor producing simple line drawings, which will provide more scope and flexibility than pictures. As the activity unfolds, so the collections of line drawings develop alongside the task and child.

Both pictures and line drawings can be used to make choices, sequence activities and convey needs. This particular communication mode mainly uses the visual sense, but should also be supported by the auditory pathway.

Picture and symbol systems

These systems have been established since the late 1980s as a substitute for speech or provide additional support to speech. They are graphic representations of an object, concept, idea or message, and represent a more advanced mode of communication. Symbols may be concrete, in the form of pictures and line drawings, or more abstract, using a formal symbol system. Formal systems include Rebus, Blissymbols, Makaton, Picture Exchange Communication System (PECS), Picture Communication Symbols (PCS), Braille and Moon (see pages 44–6). All may be embossed, although usually only Braille and Moon come in this form. Symbols rely on the use of our visual and tactile senses.

Moon

A	B	C	D	E	F
Λ	∪	C	⊃	Γ	Γ
G	**H**	**I**	**J**	**K**	**L**
ʔ	o	I	J	<	L
M	**N**	**O**	**P**	**Q**	**R**
⅂	N	O	⌣	⊃	\
S	**T**	**U**	**V**	**W**	**X**
/	—	U	V	∧	>
Y	**Z**	**and**	**the**	**!**	**?**
⌐	Z	S	∸	!	?
:	**,**	**.**	**'**	**(**	**)**
•	•	••	•	••	••

Braille

●○ ○○ ○○	●○ ●○ ○○	●● ○○ ○○	●● ○● ○○	●○ ○● ○○	●● ●○ ○○	●● ●● ○○	●○ ●● ○○	○● ●○ ○○
A	B	C	D	E	F	G	H	I

○● ●● ○○	●○ ○○ ●○	●○ ●○ ●○	●● ○○ ●○	●● ○● ●○	●○ ○● ●○	●● ●○ ●○	●● ●● ●○	●○ ●● ●○
J	K	L	M	N	O	P	Q	R

○● ●○ ●○	○● ●● ●○	●○ ○○ ●●	●○ ●○ ●●	○● ●● ●○	●● ○○ ●●	●○ ○● ●●	●● ○● ●●
S	T	U	V	W	X	Y	Z

Deafblind alphabet

Selection of symbols

Word	PCS	Rebus	Makaton	Bliss
boat				

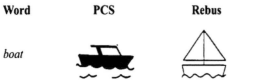

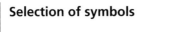

Rebus (Writing with Symbols)

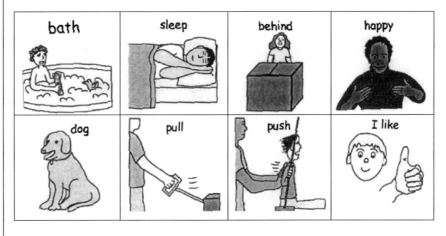

PECS

bath	sleep	behind	happy
dog	pull	push	I like

PCS (inclusive writer)

maths	writing	home	dinner
man	woman	teacher	drink

Braille and Moon

Both Braille and Moon are intended for blind or deafblind people. Braille is a system of embossed dots based on the domino representation; the dots are combined and arranged to represent letters, words and numerals. Moon is a system of only 36 raised shapes based on the standard alphabet and is much easier to learn than Braille.

Symbols require more understanding than objects and the more abstract the symbols become, the greater the level of literacy the child requires to access them.

REBUS

Developed from the American Peabody reading Programme. Contains 950 black and white symbols that are clear and simple. Rebus symbols are used in the 'Writing with Symbols' software available from Widget.

PECS (Picture Exchange Communication System)

The system includes over 1,200 coloured pictures covering broad categories and are available from Pyramid Educational Consultants. PECS is available on CD and other resources include interactive books, lesson materials and visual timetable kits. This system is popular with children with ADHD and autism and uses symbols for emotions and needs.

PCS (Picture Communication Symbols)

There is a vocabulary of over 3,000 coloured symbols and is available from Winslow Publishing. The symbols are simple and clear and are used in the Boardmaker and Inclusive Writer software.

Makaton symbols

This system was originally based on Rebus symbols but later developed in its own right. The vocabulary is clear and bold and contains over a 1,000 black and white symbols.

Blissymbols

This system contains approximately 2,500 black and white symbols that are very simple. However, it is not very popular as the symbols are quite abstract. It is available from Handicom using the 'Blissymbols for Windows' software.

Objects of reference

This is a system through which objects are used to represent activities, places and people. Ockelford (1993) describes objects of reference as objects that have special meanings assigned to them: they stand for something in the same way that words do. Just like words, objects of reference can mean anything we want them to – a cup or spoon may be used to represent drinking or eating, a carpet tile stuck to a door may serve to identify a room, and tactile badges or bracelets may be used to distinguish people. Abstract shapes can be used to convey feelings and preferences. An objects of reference system involves visual, auditory, tactile, gustatory and olfactory senses.

Objects can be used to explain the activities that will occur throughout each day, forming an object of reference timetable. Objects are presented to the child at the beginning of each activity, remain with him throughout the activity, and are put away at the end as a sign that the activity is over. This system becomes a way of explaining to the child what is happening, and later the child will learn the relevance of objects in relation to activities. In time, he will be able to choose activities using two or more objects. Any changes to planned activities or events can be explained through this system, helping children to learn consistency and overcome uncertainty about the events of their day.

Objects of reference should be carefully stored in a box to ensure they are not lost and are available when they are required. Be careful about the objects that are chosen because it is important that they can easily be replaced if lost.

For an objects of reference timetable, objects can either be placed in an oblong box that has been sub-divided or can be suspended on a rail using keyring holders. The child may transfer the objects either to their pocket or to a belt pouch, returning them to the storage box when the activity is over.

An object of reference can be a whole object or part of an object (e.g. the handle of a cup) or be a miniature object or a shape. The choice of the type of object is dependent on the ability and level of understanding of the child. Progression from whole objects to partial or miniature objects needs to be slowly and carefully introduced in order to avoid confusion and misunderstanding.

Some children have difficulties in accepting objects of reference, as they cannot tolerate handling objects without a real concrete function. Children may have difficulties accepting objects as a mode of communication. Placing objects on card or hardboard helps to resolve this intolerance.

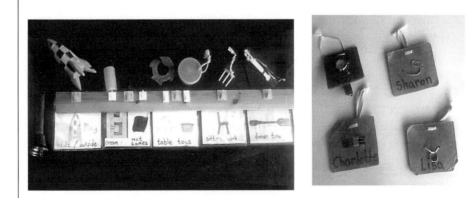

Communication Boards

Communication boards are another way of facilitating effective communication with children who are unable to use verbal communication or where speech is difficult or unclear. These are boards that display and use objects of reference, symbols, letters, words or a combination of these, and are arranged in such a way that the child is able to identify to other people what they are communicating. Communication boards may be switch-orientated using a dial or lights or, alternatively, they can be designed using cardboard. The child is asked questions and is encouraged to indicate their response through the board. The child can either operate the system by switch or by indicating to the adult through gesture or vocal response, when the adult points to the symbol or word on the board.

A communication board can be as simple or as complex as you like, however, it is important to watch out for overcrowding of symbols on the boards and ensure that symbols are not too small. A maximum number of 20 symbols per board is recommended; ideally 12 symbols is better, however, this will depend on the child. An A4-size board could easily be divided into 12 symbols/sections and be stored appropriately within a binder. This size is also easily manageable and portable.

A number of master communication boards will need to be made. These will vary from a basic needs board, including the symbols or words for happy, sad, yes, no, food, drink, biscuit, toilet, music and television. This can be extended to menu boards. Menu boards would identify a range of subjects and would link to other boards with other symbols providing more detailed information. A menu board could include key subjects such as family, home, television, music, likes, dislikes, maths and science. The family board would include names of parents, siblings, grandparents and other significant members. The home board could include rooms and favourite places.

The life story of Ruth Sienkiewicz-Mercer recounts how, as a child with multiple disabilities, she had lived in an institute in the USA for 16 years. The staff believed that she was severely intellectually impaired because she was very physically disabled and unable to speak. Finally, she succeeded in communicating with staff using facial gestures and a range of communication boards. She eventually left the institution to live in sheltered housing accommodation and is now married. The effective use of communication boards is clearly depicted in this powerful and dramatic story.

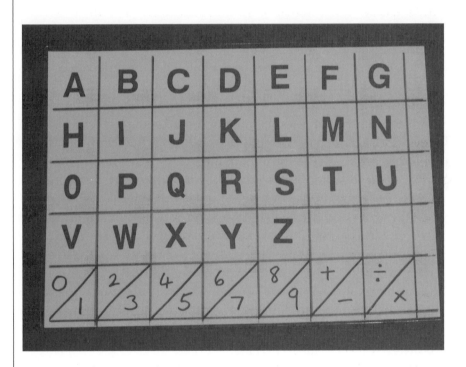

Visual or Object Timetables

A visual or object timetable assists the person who has poor communication skills to indicate preferences and to prompt and predict a sequence of events/activities, through the use of an object or shape, photograph, picture or symbol. Visual or object timetables enable the child to anticipate what is going to happen next, thus providing order, control and security. They increase the child's independence, reduce stress and enable the child to cope with change and new routines. They also provide a means to determine the completion of one activity and the actioning of another.

Visual or object timetables need to be portable, durable, adaptable and practical. They need to be in good condition, laminated, attractive and motivating. They should operate from left to right (first activity in the first left-sided box). It is important that two copies are made, in case an item is lost. Introduce the visual or object timetable by teaching the idea first. Start with one routine activity that the child knows and reinforce this with an object or picture. Make a simple timetable template or object tray.

For each activity, say the word and relate the object or picture to the event. When each activity is completed, say 'finished' and put the object or picture into a 'Finished' bin or pocket. The finished bin could be like a postbox or a pocket attached to the board. The objects or pictures can be stored in a belt pouch around the pupil until the activity is completed or left on the timetable and carried from one activity to another. It is then removed and placed in the 'finished' bin. In the beginning, avoid presenting too many pictures or symbols to the child as this can lead to confusion. Introduce more pictures in sections or chunks, such as those activities up to break-time, then lunchtime and then the afternoon. Reinforce each section before moving onto the next section (i.e. this is what we have done and this is what we are doing next) and introduce each session with a brief discussion about what is about to happen. At the end of the day the activities can be reintroduced and reinforced. A photocopy of the timetable can be placed in the home-school book, so that further communication can be continued at home with the parents. Always present the word with the symbol.

A suggested size could be 90cm × 15cm with cards 8cm × 10cm. The card could be folded over to separate the morning and afternoon sessions. This template could be portable or fixed on the wall. On the back of the card could be a 'Finished' pocket.

It is important to consider the child's level of understanding when devising a visual timetable. Start with a photograph, then picture before using symbols. Put the word under or above the photograph, picture or symbol. Again start with the real object before using miniatures or shapes. Always start with the concrete before the abstract.

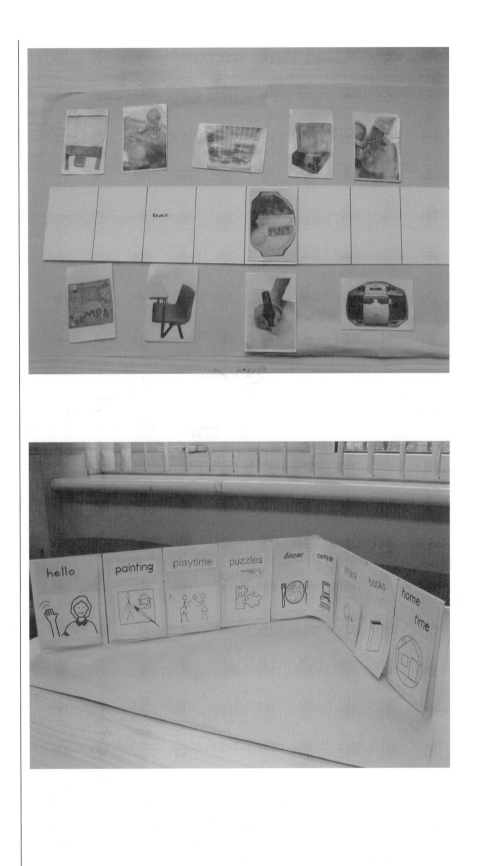

3

Personal Passports

The concept of personal passports was developed by Sally Millar, a communication therapist based at the CALL Centre in the University of Edinburgh. Sally's book (2003) gives some further information. Personal Passports are short biographies of the child, presented in a personalized and interesting way that contains sufficient information about the child and his needs, but at the same time is jargon-free.

They are written in the first person and should be read as if the child was talking to others about himself. They should contain all the basic information required to work with the child and include general information (e.g. name, address, age, school), medical condition, communication skills, preferences and dislikes, and any other relevant information that others need to know (e.g. what to do in the case of emergency). Personal passports should be read by all those working with the child, including coach escorts, drivers and supply teachers. They can be placed in the child's bag or on the back of a wheelchair.

Personal Passports provide important information about the individual, who cannot speak for himself, for the purpose of facilitating communication and understanding. The Passport becomes the voice of the child. They provide a means of facilitating a consistency of support and understanding about the individual and are valuable tools during transition periods (i.e. starting a new school or working with new staff). When writing Personal Passports it is important to involve parents, as they are essential sources of information and knowledge about their child. Personal Passports need to be stored digitally, so that they can be updated every year, after the individual's birthday. The birthday often dates the Personal Passport record, which is a positive feature in that it guarantees that information held within them is fairly accurate and appropriate.

Personal Passports need to be presented in a humorous and interesting way so that the reader will remember its content and will remain focused.

The layout of the Personal Passport should include the following sections:

Hello
Name, age, school, mother, father, siblings, address, religion, languages spoken in the home, family's origin, photograph of the family.
My school
Name of teacher and support assistant, class number, best friends and how they get to school and the names of their coach driver and bus escort.
My body
Physical disabilities, equipment used (i.e. wheelchair, standing frame, wedge).

How I see and hear

Level of vision (distance, near, upper and lower visual field, peripheral vision, colour vision, wears spectacles), level of hearing (conductive, sensori-neural, high/low frequency sounds, hearing aids).

Communication

Yes and No response, speech, pictures or symbols understood, signing, general level of understanding to answer questions and to make needs known.

Things I like

Activities, food, drink, music, television films.

Things I dislike

Activities, food, drink, music, television films.

Self care

Help and equipment required for basic needs and how they communicate these needs, including toileting, dressing, washing, eating and drinking.

Important things

Other things not mentioned such as medication, other conditions like epilepsy, feeling sad.

The front cover should be laminated and have the child's name, photograph and publication date. The Personal Passport should be all in bold, large print (suggested font and size–Arial 18 points), double spaced and placed in a spiral binder so that pages can be replaced as the Passport is updated.

Communication books

Communication books are albums of photographs, pictures, symbols or words that are used to prompt and indicate activities and feelings of the child to significant others. The child points to a picture to indicate their needs and the adult points to the picture to reinforce activities and events. These pictures may be the same picture that were used for the visual timetable.

These books have been successfully used with autistic children in particular, but are also effective for all children with complex needs. These albums should consist of no more than 20 pictures, approximately 10.5cm × 10cm (six pictures from A4). Pictures, photographs and symbols need to be well contrasted and simply presented in the same way the visual timetable. They need to be laminated and loosely bound with a tag so that they can be attached to a belt around the child. This mode of communication was promoted in the film *Mercury Rising*, when Bruce Willis needed to help an autistic boy.

Tips for engaging in communication

1 Alert the child to your presence by touching his hand or shoulder, as well as using your voice.

2 Identify who you are by using a personal object of reference.

3 Alert the child to forthcoming activity (e.g. touch his lip before giving food or drink).

4 Introduce the activity by using an object of reference or picture.

5 Discuss the activity with the child, always reinforcing actions with speech, objects of reference or sensory clues.

6 Review what you have done so that the child can have additional time to assimilate information.

7 Let the child know when an activity is over, using the finished sign and/ or by putting the object away.

Key points

● Believe that all children have communication skills and seek to discover them.

● Establish effective Intervenor skills and decide the best position of intervention.

● Identify the child's 'Yes' and 'No' responses.

● Select and establish effective communication strategies and methods to empower the child to make successful interactions and to communicate their needs and to provide a future basis for developing communication skills.

● Use visual or object timetable to help children to organize, predict and anticipate their day.

● Publish personal passports that will inform all those working with the child.

---

4 Facilitating the use of sensory information and developing a multi-sensory curriculum

Bradley is seven years old. He was born prematurely and experienced a brain haemorrhage when he was three days old. He has cerebral palsy with a right-sided hemiparesis. He has a bilateral right hemianopia with optic atrophy and is registered blind. He also has a sensori-neural hearing loss, his left ear being worse than his right ear. An MRI scan showed that he has little brain activity on his left hemisphere with only patches of activity on his right hemisphere. Despite these difficulties, Bradley enjoys life tremendously. He is able to speak, and to ask and respond to questions. Bradley can count up to ten and identifies colours. He walks independently and can feed and drink for himself. He loves being with peers who are not disabled and attends a mainstream school, receiving full-time support. He actively participates in the Literacy Hour and Numeracy Hour and works alongside his peers for all activities. Recently he went to the Millennium Dome and had an enjoyable and stimulating time.

'A sensory curriculum should be part of a whole school curriculum or learning experience for multi-sensory impaired pupils. It covers the development of the senses of vision, hearing, taste, smell (olfactory), touch (haptic) and bodily experiences (kinesthetic and propreoceptive). It also covers the development of the integration of all these senses to form a multi-sensory approach for the child to use in learning situations.'

Longhorn (1992)

Facilitating the use of sensory information and developing a multi-sensory curriculum is a vital ingredient in the education of children with multiple disabilities. This should not be viewed in isolation to learning but be interpreted within it. In order to facilitate the use of sensory information and develop a multi-sensory curriculum, we first need to understand the function of the cerebral cortex and how sensory information is processed and used. Once a clearer understanding has been reached we can then develop skills and appreciate the complexity of the learning process.

Function of the brain

There are four main components of the brain. They are the cerebrum, the cerebellum, the thalamus, and the brain stem and spinal cord.

The cerebrum is the most highly developed and largest part of the brain and is divided into two hemispheres. The cerebrum is highly organized and is arranged in areas that relate to different parts of

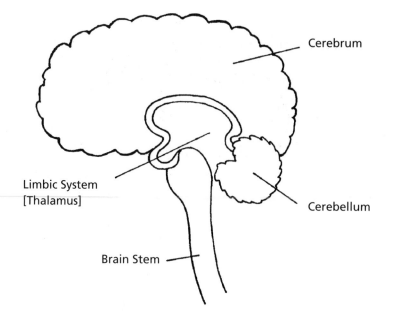

Cerebrum

Limbic System
[Thalamus]

Cerebellum

Brain Stem

the body and to different needs. The brain looks like a mass of grey jelly and is very soft. It is protected in a hard, bony case the skull.

The two hemispheres are known as the right and left hemispheres and function in different ways. The right hemisphere controls the left side of the body and the left hemisphere controls the right side of the body.

The left hemisphere is responsible for the analytical side of brain function, processes information sequentially and specializes in recognizing the parts that make up the whole. It also processes verbal information and logical thought. It recognizes that one stimulus comes before another stimulus, and it separates out the parts. This hemisphere processes subject matters including language, writing, mathematics and science.

The right hemisphere is responsible for the motor component of speech and for bringing together all the sensory information from the left hemisphere, especially visual and spatial images. It is holistic in its function and is responsible for the thinking mode. This hemisphere processes subject matters including music, art and creative thought.

Efficient processing of information requires access to both hemispheres. Problems occur when a child is unable fully to utilize either or both of them.

The cerebral cortex is the thick wrinkled layer over the outside of the cerebrum. The cerebral cortex is divided into four lobes and they are identified as follows:

● *Frontal*: responsible for speech, memory and complex thought.
● *Perinatal* (top): responsible for touch, taste, controlling body movements and sensations.
● *Temporal* (sides): responsible for hearing, smell, auditory and visual memory.
● *Occipital* (back): responsible for visual cortex, reading and visual perception.

56

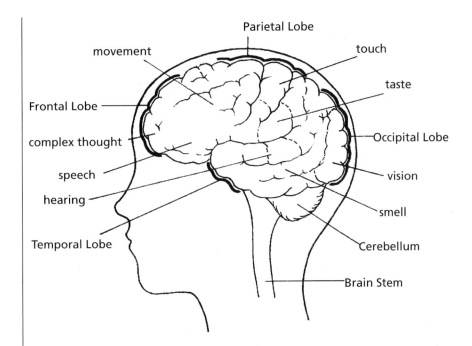

The cerebellum is below the cerebrum and is mainly responsible for controlling muscle coordination. It sends out signals which produce unconscious movements in muscles so that posture and balance are maintained, and it acts to coordinate body movements within the brain.

The thalamus is in the centre or the inner part of the cerebrum. This is a collection of specialized nerve centres, which connect to the brain, and is like a telephone exchange for the cerebrum. It controls our thoughts regarding eating, sleeping and body temperature, and is invariably linked to other senses (especially smell), behaviour and the organization of memory. It is part of the limbic system – that part of the brain that deals with emotions, mood, behaviour and evocative memory.

All visual information passes through the thalamus and limbic system by visual tracts and then returns to this area for a second time after it has been to the visual cortex. The thalamus links visual information to evocative smell, body temperature and behaviour, and integrates visual memory and perception from the hippocampus. Body temperature is regulated by the limbic system through the hypothalamus.

The brain stem is at the base of the brain and is incorporated into the spinal cord. The spinal cord is a cylindrical column of nerve tissues which runs inside the backbone. The spinal cord acts as a two-way conductive system between the brain and the body and controls simple reflex actions. It is linked to the thalamus, the cerebellum and cerebrum. It is responsible for receiving and transmitting messages to the brain and body. The brain stem, which links the brain with the spinal cord, is responsible for gathering together incoming and outgoing messages and crossing these messages over from the right side of the brain to the left side of the body and vice versa. It contains the sleep and wakefulness centre and it is this area that is mostly affected by medication, drugs and alcohol.

For those working with children with multiple disabilities, understanding how the cerebral cortex works provides a valuable insight as to where the difficulties may lie. It is likely that a child whose difficulties lie in the frontal lobe will have problems with speech, memory and complex thought. Professionals should be aware of the potential difficulties arising from a child's medical condition and relate these to the functioning of the cerebral cortex in order to plan appropriate intervention strategies.

Visual perceptual difficulties

Visual perception is the brain's ability to interpret and use information that is seen – our internal construction of the world or the ability to use visual information to recognize, recall and discriminate. This is an active process and involves scanning the environment by carefully positioning the eyes and positioning the body accordingly. The interpretation and processing of visual information is not only linked to the visual tracts and visual cortex, but is closely tied to the limbic system. Here, visual information passes backwards and forwards, checking and cross-referencing, modulating and adjusting visual information until meaning is applied and understood.

Attention deficit hyperactivity disorder (ADHD)

ADHD is linked to the failure of transmitters and receptors working within the brain. This mainly affects the frontal lobe and, as a result, children will often have difficulties with complex thought rather than with simple and basic functions.

Children with ADHD are unable to avoid being distracted from daily tasks and are often found rushing around the classroom attempting to collect as much information as possible about the world.

The child who has a hypoactivity disorder will often be distracted by his own thoughts and will end up dreaming his way through activities.

Characteristics
- may rush around the classroom
- fidgets
- interferes with other children
- easily distracted (e.g. passing car outside the classroom)
- difficulty completin.g tasks
- blurts out answers without being asked
- difficulty following instructions
- impatient, won't wait and take turns
- reluctant to stay in his chair
- impulsive and does not think about the consequences of his actions
- responds to situations in irrational, inappropriate and unacceptable ways.

Strategies:
- provide structured environments and consistent routines
- give children help in organizing and sorting all information
- be flexible in adapting the classroom for these children
- seat the children in positions that restrict distractions (e.g. the front of the class or the quiet area) or give them headphones
- differentiate work
- set realistic and obtainable objectives and expectations
- provide good role models to encourage appropriate behaviour
- maintain eye contact with the child during the issuing of instructions
- give clear and concise directions, avoiding multiple commands
- repeat requests in a calm and positive manner and do not raise your voice or be confrontational in your approach
- be aware that medication has proven effective with some children
- give very specific praise when you catch them being good
- give advance warning when something is about to happen or finish
- arrange the room in a way that minimizes distraction
- set short, achievable, targets and give instant rewards when the child remains on task
- present text in a large font and in a clear and uncluttered format
- keep the classroom rules clear and simple and be consistent in applying them to everyone.

Autistic spectrum disorder (ASD)

There are a number of causes for autism, which include biological, medical, psychological and behavioural factors and there is a strong genetic link. The diagnosis is based on the 'Triad of Impairment' which recognizes patterns of behaviour from early childhood that indicates an impairment of social interaction, communication and development of imagination. Autism affects four times as many boys as girls.

Characteristics:
- difficulties with social interaction
- inability to empathize with others and understand others' feelings
- may be aloof and make little attempts to make friends
- use of inappropriate greetings
- may become distressed and confused
- difficulties with communication skills
- avoids eye contact and unable to interpret facial expressions, gesture and body language
- some never develop speech, others experience a language delay some use repetitive, learnt phrases
- tend to interpret information literally and find humour difficult to understand
- difficulties with thought and imagination
- find play difficult, fixating on particular toys
- interested in objects more than people and can see people as objects

- distressed by changes in routine
- hand flapping, rocking or spinning may be exhibited
- erratic sleeping patterns displayed
- sensitive to noise, smell, taste and touch
- may use aggressive behaviour and injure themselves
- may be hyperactive
- present unusual gait and may walk on tip-toe
- displays irrational fears or phobias
- some have a special creative or mathematical skill
- hyperacuisis – sensitive to certain noises (i.e. clapping)
- prospagnosia – facial blindness.

Strategies to help overcome ASD:
- provide a structured environment and consistent routines
- provide them with personal space
- use visual timetables and a communication book
- consider lighting and noise
- provide one instruction at a time
- keep verbal instructions clear and brief
- teach humour and jokes
- prepare them for changes in advance
- be calm and flexible
- encourage eye contact but don't demand it (reward them when they do)
- provide clear boundaries
- use of coloured overlays or/and prescribed coloured spectacle
- an specialist visual assessment is often critical in improving visual and sensory difficulties.

Asperger's Syndrome (AS)

Asperger's Syndrome is viewed as the higher-ability aspect of the autistic spectrum.

Characteristics:
- difficulties with social relationships, reading signals and interacting with others
- monotonous speeches about topics of interest
- avoids eye contact
- enjoys obsessive, repetitive routines and re-occupations
- difficulties with communication – speak fluently but disregard listener's interests
- difficulties with social imagination, imaginative play and flexible thinking
- difficulties with abstract thought.
- naïve and gullible
- unaware of others' feelings
- easily upset by changes
- overly sensitive to loud sounds
- physically awkward in sports
- tendency to fidget and rock
- Prospagnosia – facial blindness.

Strategies to help overcome AS:

- be flexible
- maintain clear structures and consistent routines
- prepare them for changes in advance
- have high expectations
- be calm and never shout
- use clear and concise instructions
- use visual timetables
- use concrete equipment
- use a buddy system
- use a computer
- apply rules consistently
- use of coloured overlays or/and prescribed coloured spectacles.

Dyslexia

This is a specific learning difficulty that results in the brain being unable to segregate and then integrate information. It is caused by malfunctions in the frontal and occipital lobes, affecting the central executive area (attention, planning, sequencing, checking); phonological loop (speech production and perception) and vasio-spatial sector (right hemisphere-space and colour). Evidence is growing that other parts of the brain may also be involved. The aetiology of dyslexia is a result of family history, slow and prolonged birth and genetic bio-chemistry. Many dyslexics have attributes linked to art, drama, music and sport.

There are three distinct, but often overlapping, areas of difficulty:

1 difficulty with reading (dyslexia)
2 difficulty with writing (dysgraphia) and
3 difficulty with numbers (dyscalculia).

Characteristics:

- poor short-term memory
- difficulty with sequencing and processing information
- high-frequency word errors (the, and, when)
- tiredness
- poor comprehension
- slow reading speed
- difficulty finding the right word for the right situation
- organization problems
- behaviour issues related to frustration
- difficulties with visual persistence and refreshment of images
- word inaccuracy
- decoding, leading to comprehension problems
- lack of dominant eye (including possible eye confusion difficulty, which eye should track – the sides of the brain have failed to talk to each other).

Strategies to help overcome dyslexia:
- make use of flow charts, pictures and diagrams
- use a dictaphone and alternative ways of recording
- provide key word lists
- provide a reading line (i.e. ruler) or crowding frame
- tactile spelling patterns
- use a structured multi-sensoryphonic programme (i.e. THRASS)
- allow extra time
- use praise effectively
- use coloured overlays or prescribed coloured spectacles
- use a task lamp
- use a visual tracking magnifier or typoscope.

Dysgraphia (Writing)

Characteristics:
- poor handwriting and letter formation
- messy handwriting with frequent crossings out
- several attempts at single words
- confuse similar letters (i.e. b, d, p, q, m, w)
- odd spelling errors
- some write backwards
- grammar errors and
- copying difficulties.

Strategies to help overcome dysgraphia:
- use a dictaphone and alternative ways of recording
- use a structured programme (i.e. THRASS)
- allow extra time
- use praise effectively
- use a multi-sensory approach
- use coloured overlays or prescribed tinted spectacles and
- use a task lamp.

Dyscalculia

Dyscalculia is an inability to process, understand, assimilate mathematical concepts and numbers. The global definition of this condition is unclear, and there is controversy over the existence of this condition due to the lack of research that has been conducted.

Characteristics:
- difficulty with time and time management (late or early)
- numeral reversals
- poor mental arithmetic
- inconsistent computation
- difficulty reading and writing numbers
- inability to learn to rote count.
- confusion with left and right orientation
- difficulties with money

- cannot remember names and faces
- problems with sequences
- difficulties learning tables, symbols and order to do things.

Strategies to help overcome dyscalculia:
- always explain a new concept step-by-step
- use concrete equipment
- use pictures and visual information
- use multi-sensory methods (i.e. tracing numbers in the sand)
- ask them to tell you the calculation process
- use the computer
- use a calculator
- allow extra time
- make use of mnemonics (e.g. Percy the square)
- cover one eye (after trying each of the eyes)
- use of coloured overlays or/and prescribed coloured spectacles.

Dyspraxia

Dyspraxia is an inability to process information and is rooted in a fault in the vestibular and proprioceptive system. Often these children become trapped by faulty processing of motor organization, so that although they want to go one way, their body initially processes information that takes them in an opposite direction. Dyspraxia results when part of the brain has failed to mature properly. Dyspraxia derives from the Greek prefix 'Bad', and praxis which means 'learned ability to carry out sequences of coordinated movements'. In many cases of dyspraxia altering the visual pathway improves spatial awareness. Portwood (1999) has provided good research and advice in screening and suggestions for effective strategies.

Characteristics:
- problems achieving normal milestones in sitting up, crawling and walking
- does not complete tasks
- poor directional skills and inability to estimate speed and distance
- changes dominance
- poor laterality and places shoes on wrong feet
- knocks things over
- limited ability to concentrate and listen
- delayed language acquisition
- coordination problems
- difficulties holding a pencil and handwriting is messy
- poor organization skills and difficulties following sequential instructions
- poor social and interpersonal skills
- difficulties getting dressed or very slow
- difficulties throwing and catching balls
- feeding problems
- difficulties understanding spatial concepts
- messy eater

4

- slow response at doing things
- children complain they dislike PE and get their things stolen
- prospagnosia – facial blindness, facial recognition problems, emotional recognition difficulties
- difficulties with visual persistence and refreshment of images, creates difficulty in tracking balls.

Strategies to help overcome dyspraxia:
- provide laterality markers to help distinguish the left side from the right side, back and front, and give the child additional support in organising his movements
- regular and consistent motor exercises focusing on hand-eye/feet coordination
- allow extra time to complete work
- encourage buddy support
- limit the amount of copying from the board
- breakdown activities into small steps
- minimize distraction
- give clear instructions
- using hedgehog balls (soft plastic spikes) makes catching easier
- playing balloon tennis
- playing tiddlywinks
- for exams provide additional time, an amanuensis and rest periods
- use of coloured overlays or/and prescribed coloured spectacles these may need to be modified in different lighting conditions
- regular and consistent motor exercises focusing on hand-eye/feet coordination.

Oral dyspraxia

Characteristics:
- fussy or faddy eaters with strong food preferences
- prefer smooth-textured food
- resistant to eat lumpy and crunchy food
- prefer dry food (i.e. chips, crisps, fish fingers).

Strategies to help overcome oral dyspraxia:
- keep to two types of food and gradually increase the choice
- introduce food at snack time first before main meal.
- make sure the other food type is smooth
- have a drink after each mouthful
- participate in food play (i.e. put food of different textures on different body parts)
- play games for blowing and breath direction exercises.

Visual Link Stress Syndrome (also known as Meares-Irien Syndrome Visual Stress or Visual Dyslexia)

This condition involves symptoms of eyestrain and visual perception distortions when reading, which can be alleviated with coloured filters or spectacles. This discovery was first reported by Meares (1980) and later Irien (1991) and has been further developed by Evan (2001), Wilkins (2002) and Jordan (1998).

Jordan (1998) argues that this visual link stress affects all our sensory system, including not only vision, but also hearing, taste, balance, mobility, touch and smell. By changing the processing of the visual pathway through the use of colour, these other senses are improved and become stronger and sensitive. Strength is also improved.

Wilkins (1991) has found in studies that about 50 per cent of normal school children prefer a coloured overlay as improving the clarity of text and 20 per cent continued to use them long term. These figures were improved using coloured spectacles with broad spectrum filter lenses measured by the Intuitive Colorimeter.

Jordan (2005) found in a research study in a Scottish primary school of eight to nine year olds that 25 per cent of the 111 sample had visual perceptual distortions. Of this sample many described some of characteristic as described below. However, he found that 87 per cent of those pupils who used a Hoya Vdex Precise Band Filter lenses measured by the Orthoscopics Read Eye had normal perception.

Evans (2001) considers that visual stress may be linked to vergence, accommodation and saccades. He therefore prescribes accurate vision assessments, eye exercises and lenses refraction as the first line treatment before diagnosis and identification.

Characteristics:
- vibration or movement of letters or words (i.e. they turn around, disappear, move up and down, spin, change shape)
- experience headaches or complains that their eyes hurt
- problems associated with glare from paper
- slow reading speed and reading errors
- sore eyes when reading
- poor concentration
- loses their place when reading
- word omissions
- rubbing eyes and excessive blinking
- double vision (diplopia)
- balance, posture or walking may be poor or awkward
- spatial awareness is poor
- intermittent blurring of letters or words
- letter inversions and reversals
- word and letter displacement/disappear
- word/letter metamorphosis – words and letters change shape or size
- poor balance
- prospagnosia – facial blindness

- asthenopia – experience headaches and pain when reading and viewing images
- scotomas – parts of visual images that are missing or patchy vision
- difficulties with visual persistence and refreshment of images
- glare problems.

Strategies to help overcome Visual Link Stress Syndrome:
- using print on different coloured paper
- providing coloured tinted spectacles that have been prescribed by a specialist optometrist using specialist equipment (i.e. Intuitive Colorimeter and the Orthoscopics Read Eye); these systems are very different – the Colorimeter uses subjective colour and therefore has a limited range, the Read eye uses additive colour and is the gold standard; coloured lenses are different, too, if there is no success using the Colorimeter it is worth pursuing the Read eye
- use of a visual tracking magnifier (Desktop) this is also very useful in screening
- using coloured overlays available in ten colours (rose, orange, yellow, lime, turquoise, aqua, blue, purple, pink and grey)
- PAT Light – this is like an angle-poised lamp, but can be adjusted to mix colours together to find the desired colour preference (orthoscopics).
- use a flatscreen monitor rather than a CRT screen
- use a coloured background on the computer
- coloraid – overlay clip-on spectacles – useful to ascertain whether tinted spectacles would be beneficial before purchase (available from ioo sales)
- eye exercises.

Tests to diagnose Visual Link Stress Syndrome include:
- Thompson City Coloured Overlay Screen Pro – provides a computerized version of the Wilkins Rate of Reading Test. Prints out a plastic overlay. Prints out a report. Test for tinted spectacles (Thompson Software).
- Thompson Coloured Tinter – tests and configures the computer display to approximate colour background and text (Thompson Software).
- Rate of Reading Test (Wilkins) – measures the improvement in reading fluency within a chosen colour. There is a reading and a non-reading test component for non-readers. The test uses a passage of common words in random order, that are familiar to most poor readers. They are in random order to prevent guessing and because the text is meaningless, readers are unaware of errors. Materials can be enlarged without altering the validity of the test (ioo Sales).
- Visual Dyslexia Screening Test (Jordan) – a small booklet containing a checklist of 25 questions (Orthoscopics).
- Visual Dyslexia Assessment kit (Jordan) – CD-Rom contains a series of questions that generate a report and referral letter to the GP or Optometrist (Orthoscopics).

- Reversal & Inversion Test (Jordan) – tests reversal of letters and colours (Orthoscopics).
- Pattern Glare Test (Jordan) – tests whether text and lighting are causing difficulties (Orthoscopics).
- Optimeyes Task Lamp – the optimum method of assessing colour for teachers, however, if this method does not work then colour does not improve the condition for this specific child.

Prosopagnosia

This newly discovered condition is described as facial blindness and the damage is located in the temporal lobe of the brain. Some children with dyslexia, dyspraxia and autism have been known to have this condition. It is useful to ask them what they see while they are looking at someone's nose.

Characteristics:
- avoid looking at faces
- physical pain when looking at faces
- facial distortions occur resulting in facial parts being occluded or missing or facial image disfiguration
- misunderstanding of facial emotions.

Strategies to overcome prosopagnosia
- alter the visual processing through the use of prescribed tinted spectacles.

Left-side dominance (left-handedness)

Children with a left-side dominance demonstrate that they favour the right side of the brain over the left side. The right hemisphere of the brain holds artistic talent and imagination, while the left side is more responsible for practical abilities and logical thinking.

It is considered that those children with a preference towards their left side tend to be more creative, musical and perceptive than those with a right-side dominance. Many are found to be highly intelligent and are more likely to demonstrate genius qualities. These children think more holistically and are not necessarily good logical thinkers. Writing and the use of certain pieces of equipment, such as scissors and cutlery are initially difficult.

Strategies:
- make sure that the correct technique of tripod grasp of the pen is maintained
- for writing, show children how to turn the paper away from them up to a 45-degree angle; giving them a slightly higher seat/lower table may help

- there is a wide variety of specialist stockists from whom you can buy appropriate left-handed pieces of equipment (e.g. scissors, cutlery, watches).

Role of an optometrist

A test by an optometrist includes refraction (test for lenses), acuity (ability to see objects at distance and near), tests of the health of the eyes and basic tests of ocular motor function (how well the eye muscles work together). The following tests can be provided and are particularly important for reading difficulties.

It is best to ask an optometrist whether they could do the following tests before booking an appointment: Mallett Fixation Disparity Test, Fusional Reserves at near, accommodation lag, coloured overlay testing, tinted spectacles prescription. If they are unable to do the test, they should be able to refer someone. For further information contact the Institute of Optometrists.

For further information regarding a visual multi-sensory assessment contact Orthoscopics.

The sensory system

Vision (visual)
Vision can be divided into three sections: the orbit, optic nerve and visual cortex. Visual problems can occur in one or all three areas and many children who are multiple disabled may be affected in all three.

The orbit (or outer part of the eye) is the first visual window to receive information and contains many parts that collectively act as a refractive mechanism to view the world. They include the cornea, iris, pupil, lens, retina, macula, aqueous humour and vitreous body (see Glossary and below).

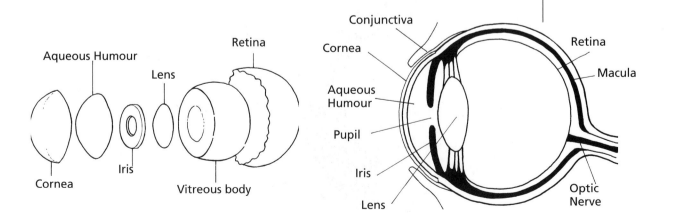

There are many eye conditions which professionals may come into contact with, including:

- myopia (shortsight)
- hypermetropia (longsight)
- amblyopia (lazy eye)
- stabismus (squint)
- anirida (absence of the iris)
- astigmatism (mis-shapen cornea)
- coloboma (keyhole-shape pupil)
- cataracts (opaque lens)
- glaucoma (faulty drainage of aqueous fluid)
- retinal dystrophy, retinitis pigmentosa and macular degeneration (degeneration of the retina)
- retinal dysplasia (failure of the retina to develop)
- hemaeopia (loss of the half side of vision of each eye) and
- nystagmus (involuntary horizontal or vertical movements of the eyes).

Visual problems include loss of central and peripheral vision, as well as patchy or scatoma vision (black spots).

The optic nerve is a very complicated area and consists of optic tracts that cross over at the optic chiasma. It is responsible for placing images up the right way, three-dimensional perception and transmitting information to the visual cortex.

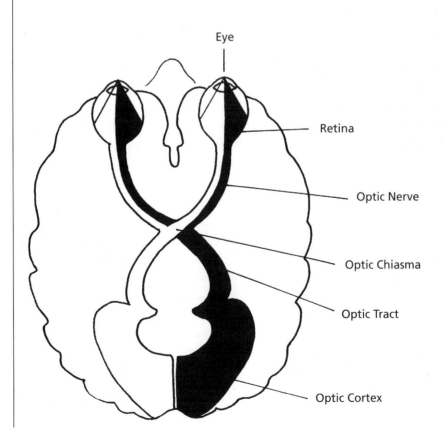

The visual cortex organizes visual information and gives it the form that we understand. If faulty, these areas cannot be fully repaired by surgery, unlike the orbit, which can be either fully or partially repaired. Optic nerve atrophy and cerebral visual impairment (cortical visual impairment) are the two most common eye conditions.

Cerebral visual impairment results in a visual performance that is highly variable, a short visual attention span and a disorganized visual picture of the world. Many children who are multiple disabled have damage to the visual cortex, with other associated orbit problems. This condition is challenging for an adult and makes it very difficult for a child to organize the world.

Causes of visual impairment include prematurity at birth (retinopathy of prematurity), genetic and congenital defects, and diabetes, along with many unknown causes.

Spectacles are worn to correct refractive errors. These errors occur when visual images do not fall precisely on the retina. Children are prescribed lenses that are made of plastic because they are less likely to break than glass. Plastic lenses are thicker than glass lenses. The bigger the frame, the thicker the lenses will be, and lenses in square-shaped frames will be thicker than those in oval-shaped frames. Glass spectacles will be heavier than plastic ones, which for some children is an advantage, for others an irritation. Spectacles for myopia use a concave lens and spectacles for hypermetropia use a convex lens. It is important that spectacles are well maintained and clean if they are to be effective for children.

Visual stimulation

The definition of visual stimulation is when an object or person is able to attract the person's attention in order to stimulate visual exploration and attention. The main aim of visual stimulation is to stimulate the child's vision to the fullest extent in order for them to make sense of the world. In addition, children will increase their eye movements and motor development, and develop vision as a coordinating sense. The stages for teaching visual stimulation can be found on pp 75–6.

The equipment that can used for visual stimulation programmes include: mirrors (i.e. concave, convex, mosaic and magnifying mirrors, foil sheets, mirror balls); glitters (i.e. body paint, face make-up, nail polish, tinsel, shiny gloves, necklaces and bracelets, Christmas decorations, foil blankets, cartwheel spinners, slinky, sequins, diffractive panels, prisms, fluorescent materials and paint); lights (i.e. Christmas tree lights, disco lamps, torches, bubble tubes, ultraviolet lamps, voice activated lights); mechanical objects (i.e. push-along, push-down and clockwork toys); puppets; and television programmes ('Hello' available from the RNIB).

Developmental Stages of Teaching Visual Stimulation

Stage	Item	Yes	No
1	**Visual Awareness and Attention** (Shows interest in a visual stimuli and attends to it)		
	Reaction to bright light in dark room		
	Reaction to lights turned on/off		
	Turning on different strengths of light on/off		
	Flickering lights using hands/fingers		
	Reaction to hand movements illuminated by lights in front of face		
	Reaction to familiar faces close up using a bright light		
	Reaction to familiar face/hands close up in daylight		
	Reaction to bright shiny objects with/without high contrast		
	Attends to everyday objects with high contrast		
	Aware and attends to moving objects at a distance		
2	**Fixation and Focusing** (Locates objects with a purposeful gaze)		
	Fixates with corrections (eyes drift away)		
	Fixates on lights		
	Fixates and focuses on faces/hand movements		
	Fixates and focuses on bright objects with high contrast		
	Fixates and focuses on black and white patterns		
	Fixates and focuses on bright objects with low contrast		

Stage 3

Reaching (Coordinates hand and eyes to touch an object)

Reaches and touches for bright objects

	Low contrast	High contrast	Right	Front	Left
15cm					
30cm					
60cm					
90cm					

Stage 4

		Yes	No
4	**Grasping** (Coordinates hand and eyes to hold an object)		
	Holds and explores objects when placed in the hand		
	Left		
	Right		
	Holds and explores objects for short periods in the hand		
	Light		
	Heavy		
	Holds heavy objects for long periods in the hand		

Stage 5

Reaching and Grasping (Coordinates hand and eyes to touch and then holds an object)

Reaches, explores and holds objects

	Right	Front	Left	Heavy	Light	High contrast	Low Contrast
30cm							
60cm							
90cm							

4

Stage	Item								
6	**Tracking** (Follows an object from a variety of directions)								
A	Follows object or light – Centre-Right-Centre-Left-Centre								
		Bright	Dull	Light	High contrast	Low contrast	10cm	30cm	
	Large								
	Small								
B	Follows object – Centre-Up-Centre-Down-Centre								
		Bright	Dull	Light	High contrast	Low contrast	10cm	30cm	
	Large								
	Small								
C	Follows object – Centre-Diagonal Right Up-Centre-Diagonal Left Up-Centre								
		Bright	Dull	Light	High contrast	Low contrast	10cm	30cm	
	Large								
	Small								
D	Follows object – Centre-Diagonal Right Down-Centre-Diagonal Left Down-Centre								
		Bright	Dull	Light	High contrast	Low contrast	10cm	30cm	
	Large								
	Small								
E	Follows object or light – Centre-Zigzag Right-Centre-Zigzag Left-Centre								
		Bright	Dull	Light	High contrast	Low contrast	10cm	30cm	
	Large								
	Small								
F	Follows object or light – Centre-Circle Right-Centre-Circle Left-Centre								
		Bright	Dull	Light	High contrast	Low contrast	10cm	30cm	
	Large								
	Small								
7	**Scanning and Searching** (Looks for an object and locates it)								
	Locates an specific object from others								
		Bright	Dull	Light	High contrast	Low contrast	30cm	60cm	90cm
	Large								
	Small								
8	**Accommodation** (Able to locate moving objects from near to distance/distance to near)								
						Yes		No	
	Blinks at flashing lights								
	Looks at lights near and distance								
	Shifts gaze from near to varying distances								
	Follows a moving adult								
	Perceives 3D objects from near to distance								
9	**Visual Discrimination** (Distinguishes visual stimuli and their attributes)								
A	Gazes and attends to the following high-contrast items								

Gazes and attends to the following high-contrast items

People	Patterns	Shapes	Black & White Pictures
Coloured Pictures	Photographs (no background)		Photographs
Symbols			

B   Matches items

Object to Object	Pattern to Pattern	Shape to Shape	Object to Black & White Picture
Black & White Picture to Black & White Picture		Coloured Picture to object	
Coloured Picture to Coloured Picture		Photograph (no background) to Photograph (no background)	
Photograph to Photograph		Symbol to Symbol	

Hearing (auditory)

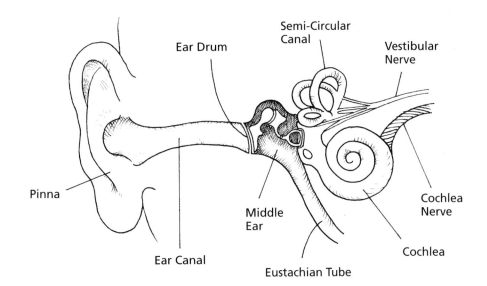

The outer ear
This consists of the pinna (ear flap) and auditory canal. This part of the ear gathers and directs sound waves along the auditory canal towards the ear drum.

The middle ear
This comprises the eardrum (tympanic membrane) and a collection of tiny bones or ossicles called the malleus, incus and stapes. This is an air-filled chamber and its efficiency is compromised if fluid is present (e.g. glue ear or otitis media). Sound is transmitted from the eardrum along the ossicles to the oval window at the entrance to the cochlea, or the inner ear.

The inner ear
This is called the cochlea and contains fluid and hair cells along its snail-like shape. The movement of the hair cells generates an electrical current, which then passes along the auditory nerve to the auditory cortex.

The auditory cortex
This has a similar function to the visual cortex, except that its function is to organize and transmit what is heard. Children with problems in this area and the inner ear are referred to as having cortical auditory disturbance or cerebral auditory impairment.

Any outer and middle ear dysfunction results in a conductive hearing loss. If there is an inner ear and auditory cortex dysfunction it is known as a sensory-neural loss. If there are problems in both these areas it is known as a mixed loss. Children with multiple disabilities tend to have mainly a sensory-neural or mixed loss.

Causes of hearing loss

Conductive hearing loss
Outer ear. Malfunctions of the pinna and blockages/growths in the auditory canal.

Middle ear. Blockage of the eustachian tube caused by fluid or otitis media in the middle ear. The treatment is the insertion of grommets (a ring) placed in the tympanic membrane. Otosclerosis occurs when there is a burst eardrum caused by fluid.

Sensory-neural hearing loss
Causes of this include the following:

- anoxia
- CHARGE association
- cytomegalovirus
- measles
- meningitis
- mumps
- neo-natal jaundice
- prematurity
- rhesus incompatibility
- rubella syndrome
- toxoplasmosis
- trauma
- Usher syndrome.

Cortical auditory disturbance or cerebral auditory impairment   *Picture Communic*
Causes include:

- effects of developmental delay or break in nerves
- non-organic hearing loss
- tinnitus and
- recruitment.

Most supermarkets emit white noise to reduce sound levels and help customers focus on products rather than the noise of others. Some of this affects children with disabilities, especially those with hearing aids.

There are a variety of hearing aids available. The most common is the post-aural (behind the ear) hearing aid. They are also available in a smaller size. Others include the radio hearing aid, the button hearing aid, and body-worn aids. Few children wear button aids that fit like a button into the pinna. In mainstream schools, a combination of the post-aural and radio hearing aid is used, with the post-aural aid turned to its 'T' (loop) setting. Well-fitting ear moulds are essential if children are to receive appropriate amplification and to reduce whistling and feedback. Children require new ear moulds regularly due to the growth of the ear and feedback is common if ear moulds are ill-fitting.

Smell (olfactory)

The sensory receptors for smell are found in the roof of the nasal cavity. This is called the olfactory area and contains millions of olfactory cells or hairs. The messages are carried to the cerebral cortex and are analysed closely by the thalamus and limbic system. This connection explains why smells have such an emotional significance – for example, the smell of fresh rain on a summer's day usually makes people happy. Conversely, unpleasant smells produce revulsion and even nausea. Certain smells will bring memories of long-forgotten special occasions.

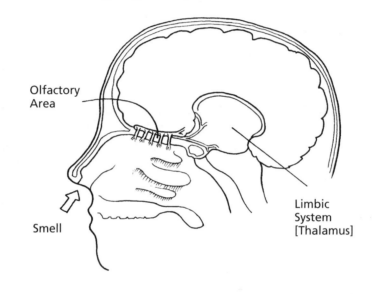

The sense of smell is the most under-used sense. It is 10,000 times more sensitive than taste. Animals rely on this sense to identify territory, locate food and recognize other animals. It has a protective function and alerts us to rotten food and poisonous substances (e.g. acid, smoke). It also continues to function during sleep, when other senses are dulled.

Children with multiple disabilities need to be helped in sorting and analysing smells and to be actively involved in choosing which ones they prefer or dislike. Careful differentiation of smells is important – if this is not managed it can lead to sensory defensiveness and projectile vomiting. Smells can be used as objects of reference, but this can present dangers if they are not related to the real thing (e.g. an apple smell used to mean a maths lesson rather than something that can be eaten).

Smell is often used by children to identify people who work with them. Therefore the habitual use of a perfume by the intervenor(s) is a useful tool of recognition and becomes a personal object of reference.

Taste (gustatory)

This is the crudest of our senses. Its exclusive role is to be a selector and appreciator of food and drink, a role that is aided by the sense of smell. The taste mechanism is triggered by chemical particles picked up in the mouth and converted into nerve impulses which are transmitted to the brain. Lying on the surface of the tongue are many hair-like projections called papillomae. Inside these are the taste buds, and they respond only to four basic tastes: sweet, sour, salt and bitter. The receptor sites for these are located on different parts of the tongue. The taste buds that are responsible for sweet tastes are at the tip of the tongue,

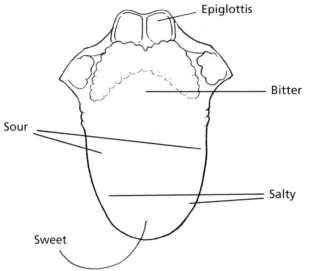

followed by salt, sour and finally bitter at the base of the tongue. Children with multiple disabilities are unable to organize these tastes and require help and structure in doing this, organising their preferences. The brain is then able to acknowledge these preferences. This is key to the teaching process. The intervenor will need to be aware of the location on the tongue of these taste buds to facilitate this learning and discriminatory skill.

Touch (tactile and haptic)

The touch receptors are located on the skin or hairs of the skin, which transmit messages to the brain via two specific pathways in the spinal cord. One pathway is for recognizing touch sensations and the other for unknown or diffuse touch sensations (pain). Touch incorporates haptic and tactile perception. Haptic perception is concerned with direct touching through the use of our hands. This is when we actively touch or when something touches us. Tactile perception is concerned with the whole body system receiving information through touch. The haptic sensation develops very early in foetal life. Touch is important for bonding, providing descriptive receptors regarding texture, shape, weight, density and size. It signals the difference between the soft touch of a child's finger and the crawling legs of a spider.

Mouthing is important for assisting tactile processing until the fingertips are able to give adequate discrimination. If mouthing is to be reduced then finger sensitivity needs to be developed.

Within this one sense are located many other senses, including sensitivity to temperature (hot, warm, cool and cold), pressure, prolonged pressure, pain, air flow regulation, weight, shape and texture. Children need help in sorting out and experiencing all these sensations if they are to fully understand the world they live in.

According to Gibson (1974) haptic information is processed in different ways. Young children attend to texture whereas older children are more interested in shape. This is important for the teacher in terms of the order in which to teach concepts, linking developmental stages with interest.

Gibson further asserted that children have difficulties differentiating between curved and straight lines when they are seen together, although they have few problems when they are presented in isolation. The difference between a single straight line and a curved line is easily distinguished. However, there are difficulties when shapes comprise both straight lines and curves. This affects the teaching of tactile modes of communication (i.e. Braille/Moon). Dots are far more difficult to recognize than shapes, although the Braille codes for e, a, l, c, k are most quickly identified.

The question of what happens to haptic information after it has been encoded is a difficult one. The answer lies in the fact that we have to remember information or we have to transform it so that it can be used. Therefore there is a natural link to the proprioceptive sense and to memory skills.

The vestibular sense

This is located in the semi-circular canals which are positioned near to the ears, and is linked to the cerebrum and cerebellum. The vestibular sense is responsible for determining which way is up, body and head balance, detecting speed (acceleration and deceleration), direction (backwards, forwards, sideways) and body positional changes. It is invariably linked with the eye muscles, as we cannot balance without hand-eye control, and helps coordinate the movements of the eyes, head and both sides of the body. This sense is sent into flux by over-spinning or excessive movement (merry-go-rounds, etc.) and the use of different drugs (excessive use of alcohol). The vestibular sense is assisted by the effective use of vision, in co-ordinating the movement of the eyes, head and both sides of the body. Children who are significantly visually impaired rely solely on the vestibular sense and any clues they can glean from their other senses including residual vision.

With children it is important to be aware of activities to develop the use of this sense. However, care should be taken as it is an extremely potent stimulation. Never use strong vestibular activities on a child with cerebral palsy or a child with epilepsy. Never increase the stimulation unless the child indicates that he is able to cope with it.

Some children have difficulty in looking up and then down again (e.g. viewing a blackboard and copying work, or using a communication aid).

Activities to improve vestibular sensation:

- provide access to a varied and balanced physical education programme
- use large play equipment (e.g. slides, roundabouts, swings)
- offer experience of different forms of transport (e.g. boats, trains, aeroplanes, tricycles, and horse-riding)
- use therapy balls and rolls, water beds and hammocks
- provide opportunities to use a trampoline, bouncy castle and a ball pool
- try rocking activities
- organize a trip to a fun fair.

The proprioceptive sense

The receptors for this sense are located inside tendons, muscles and joints and help us to coordinate their movements. This sense helps us to locate our position in space and gives us an awareness of body position, allowing us to gain skilful manipulation of hand/feet movements within a smooth synchronization.

Activities to improve proprioception:

- access to a varied and balanced physical education programme
- throwing, catching, pushing and pulling activities
- using a trampoline, ball pool and a bouncy castle
- practice in dressing and undressing
- using equipment that develops mobility skills (wedges, standing frames, gait trainers)
- swimming and horse-riding activities
- clapping
- using vibro-tactile equipment (e.g. a resonance board).
- dance activities
- interactive massage sessions.

Sensory Integration Disorders

Without organization there is chaos. Without sensory integration the sensory system bombards the cerebral cortex, resulting in disorganization and confusion. Part of the function of sensory integration is the ability to filter out unnecessary sensations and to attend to and gather information on important sensations. It is also important to sort and organise sensory information so that the person is able to make sense of it in a non-distorted manner.

The proprioceptive sense helps us to locate our position in space and gives us an awareness of body position

Tactile defensiveness

This is a heightened sensitivity to touch, movement or sounds, resulting in an excessive and adverse reaction. Children may avoid certain textures of clothes, food, sound and smells. Any or all of these may be associated with a bad experience, so that every time a child comes into contact with certain textures and objects, this experience is relived. Tactile defensiveness often affects bonding.

There are a number of reasons for tactile defensiveness, including confusion; an inability to adapt to new experiences; a lack of verbal cues; an unpleasant and uncomfortable experience; a lack of understanding; a feeling of isolation; difficulties in establishing an attachment to one person; insufficient time by the adult to cue into the child's communication system; and a feeling of being frightened. The effects are that the children feel nervous, insecure, upset and powerless.

To reduce tactile defensiveness we need to:
- Provide consistency by using the same people to teach these children, preferably teaching in the same place.
- Provide routines that children can anticipate and predict, so they can feel safe and secure.
- Alert children when communication is about to take place and provide appropriate communication modes.
- Build up tolerance levels in children by using our voice to reassure them and by gradually introducing sensory experiences.

Feeling relaxed and safe, confident not tense, and having a feeling of acceptance all reduce tactile defensiveness. Aromatherapy and interactive massage also help minimize and resolve this problem.

Under-reaction to sensory stimulation

A child with this disorder may seek out intensive sensory experiences such as rocking, body twirling, body injury and self-inflicting pain, or jumping straight-legged.

Intermittent activity level

This can occur when a child receives a mixed array of interaction varying from extremely low to high or moderate intervention level. Mood swings and erratic behaviour may occur moving from passive/withdrawn behaviour to over-active behaviours.

Coordination

Coordination problems may be demonstrated in clumsiness, difficulties with gross/fine motor control and balance.

Developmental delay

Delays in speech, language, motor skills and academic achievement may be linked to poor sensory integration.

Organization

Poor behavioural organization is often linked to sensory integration. Often these children show a lack of planning when they approach tasks. They have difficulties in adjusting to new situations and can show this through frustration, aggression, withdrawal, and poor self-esteem. They may be impulsive, lack concentration and be easily distractable. Many have difficulties calming down, unwinding and relaxing.

Poor self-concept

Encouragement, success and rewards are very important to help overcome poor self-esteem. Being in control of one's destiny anng meaningful choices and decisions facilitates self-esteem.

Stages of interaction

McInnes and Treffry (1984) suggested that there are nine stages or sequences to interaction. They are:

1 actively resists
2 passively resists
3 tolerates – co-actively (hand over hand)
4 cooperates passively
5 enjoys
6 responds cooperatively
7 leads
8 imitates
9 initiates.

When initiating interaction it is very important that careful consideration is paid to these stages. It may be necessary to work at a 'hands-off' approach if the child is resistant to touch by people, but is less resistant to touch by objects.

Body tolerance levels

Discovering the sensitivity levels of different parts of the body will determine areas of tactile tolerance and intolerance, and this will provide a useful source of information when attempting to reduce tactile defensiveness. Using a chart to plot these tolerance levels will help to ascertain areas that can and cannot be touched in order to avoid adverse reactions (see p. 84). It is likely that what will be discovered is that there are different tolerance levels for different sides of the body and also that some body parts are 'no-go areas' for touching. Body parts that are ticklish are activity resist ant areas.

Body tolerance level chart

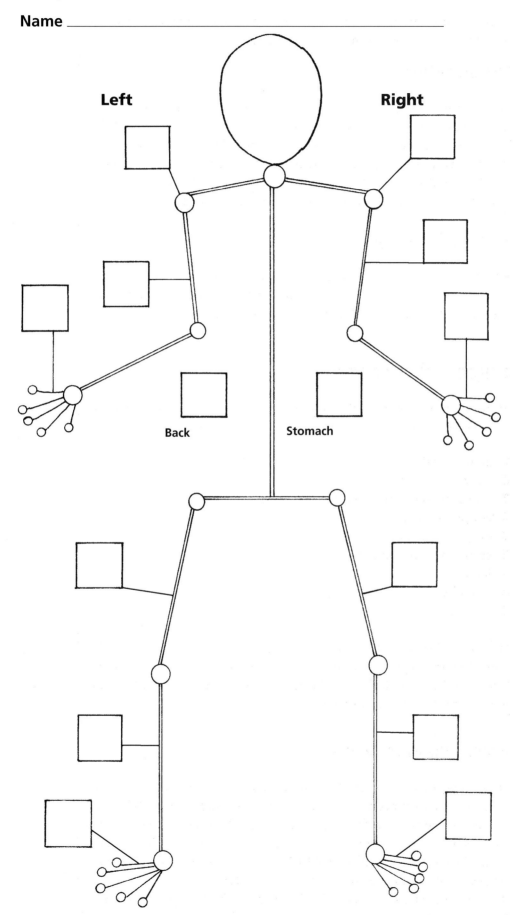

Left

Right

Back

Stomach

Aromatherapy

Aromatherapy is the inhaling of essential oils to promote health and a general sense of well-being. It can induce relaxation, invigoration, healing, alertness and sensory receptivity, and act as an anti-depressant. It is closely associated in developing the sense of smell. Aromatherapy has been found to help children overcome sensory integration difficulties and also to reduce tactile defensiveness.

The oils can be inhaled through the use of fans and burners, or by massage, or mixed in bath water. Excessive use of any of these methods can result in a sensory overdose and can be extremely dangerous. So it is important to be careful of the amount of oil used and the period of time allocated.

There are nine essential oils:

> *Lavender* (calming and relaxing): used for healing (e.g. cuts, colds, headaches, backaches and pain) and helps to relieve hyperactivity and distress.
> *Roman chamomile* (calming and relaxing): used to help stomach upsets, indigestion, eczema and toothache.
> *Bergamot* (sedating but uplifting): used as an anti-depressant and insect repellent.
> *Mandarin* (calming and gentle): used for tight skin.
> *Rosemary*: a strong stimulant.
> *Geranium*: used as an anti-depressant and for tiredness. It is wiser to avoid late evening usage.
> *Frankincense* (calming and uplifting): excellent for skin care.
> *Juniper*: useful for rheumatism and arthritis.
> *Ylang Ylang*: used as a sedative and anti-depressant and is helpful for lowering blood pressure.

Aromatherapy should not be used if the child is receiving medical treatment or if he has cancer or terminal illness (unless approved by a medical adviser). It is increasingly being used in conjunction with interactive massage and provides another tool for working with children with multiple disabilities.

Interactive massage

Massage is one method of making meaningful contact with the child. It helps to develop bonding and a close rapport with the child. It elicits communication skills, reinforces the concept of 'More' and promotes cooperation. Interactive massage relaxes and loosens stiff muscles and eases joint pains and muscle tension. It develops tactile awareness and skills, and also facilitates manual manipulation as a pre-requisite to gross and fine motor skills. It can also help to boost circulation and to eliminate toxic waste matter. Massage increases the oxytosin level (chill factor) and reduces the adrenalin level.

When providing interactive massage it is important to create the right environment, atmosphere and space, so that it can be a relaxing and beneficial experience. When conducting massage, the adult should remember to remove watches, rings and bracelets, as these may cause injury to the child. No massage should be undertaken unless training has previously been provided. Professional advice should be sought at the onset of any treatment regarding its appropriateness for the child, the suitable techniques to follow and which oils to use. It is essential, if massage is to be used in a school, that a school policy is in operation to act as a guide to staff and information to parents.

Preparing for massage:
● make sure the room is warm and the child is comfortable
● remove as many distractions as possible
● use a cue (i.e. calming music) and
● begin when everyone is quiet.

The massage:
● remember to ask the child permission to touch him
● repeat movements slowly
● always keep physical contact
● say when you have finished and
● thank him for allowing massage.

Massage can be used to enhance the teaching of all curriculum subjects. Using massage to tell stories can enhance learning, you not only hear the words of the story and see the visual imagery, but also begin to 'feel' the story and its characters. The children should always be in control and should be able to say or indicate 'No' or 'Yes'.

The Massage in Schools programme has identified a number of strokes to use with children. These can be used by adults or pupils within an interactive curriculum session. They include the following:

Eye glasses: Make three circles around the shoulder blades. Stroke out to the arms and hold.
Baker: Place hands on shoulders and make gentle movements with the palm and fingers.
Hairdresser: Place fingers on top of the hair and make cicles with the fingertips.
Hearts: Begin almost at the base of the spine, moving up with one hand on either side of the spine, move the hands upward making a heart-shaped formation and coming back down to the base of the spine. Continue making larger and larger heart formations. Note: this stroke is not on the spine.

> *Bear Walking:* Place hands on either side of the spine, almost at the bottom of the spine. Press one hand after another 'walking' up the back. When you get to the neck 'walk' back down again.
>
> *Climbing down a rope:* Kneel down to one side of the person receiving the massage. Place one hand just under the armpit. Press firmly yet gently and 'climb' hand over hand, down to the hand. Climb back up again.

Massage stories

I Hear Thunder

I hear thunder (clap on the back with flat hands).
Repeat.
Hark don't you (draw a question mark).
Repeat.
Pitter patter raindrops (make raindrops with fingertips).
I'm wet through (slide down each side of spine fingers pointing in)
So are you (hold shoulders).

The Jungle

It was a lovely sunny day (circular flat hands in a circular shape on the back with strokes to the sides, for sun rays).
We were walking through the jungle (flat hands walk up either side of the spine).
The wind was rustling through the grass (finger tips zig-zag from shoulders to base of spine).
What would I see? (draw a question mark).
First I saw a snake slithering through the grass (use the side of the hand making a curved path from base to shoulder).
Then I saw a lion with a curly mane (clawed hands draw outline of mane).
And a very tall giraffe with a long neck (flat hands move up the back into the neck).
A tiger with stripes came to say 'Hello' (draw diagonal lines with fingertips).
Until the sun went down (circular flat hand moves down to the base of back).
And we waved goodbye (waving movement back up to shoulders and hold).

For further information contact the Massage in Schools Programme.

Techniques

There are six basic techniques used in interactive massage.

They are as follows:

- *Effleurage*: movement which is mainly done with the flat of the hand, with fingers close together, with the tips of the fingers turning upwards. It has a relaxing effect.
- *Pétrissage*: This movement is applied with the balls of the thumb and/or fingers and is applied to soft tissue immediately underneath the skin.

Supporting Children

- *Taptement*: These are fine quick movements by the fingers of one or both hands.
- *Kneading*: This is used on soft tissue that has no bone underneath it and its action is very similar to that of kneading bread. The movement is to pick the tissue up and away from the bone and to roll it back with squeezing or pressure action.
- *Cupping*: This is a quick movement achieved with the hands in a cupping position and is a technique mainly used on the back. The finger joints are straight and the thumb is brought in closely to create an almost airtight formation. When the hand is brought down it creates a vacuum which sucks the blood towards the surface.
- *Hacking*: This is achieved with the edge of the hand, with the muscles of the hand in a relaxed position and is similar to a karate chop action.

Reflexology

This is a method of treatment whereby finger pressure is applied to pressure points in the feet and hands, which are massaged to bring about relaxation and relief. Those who operate this technique hold the belief that these pressure points are points of energy affecting the well-being of the whole body. These pressure points on the feet and hands reflect all the parts of the body, both internal and external organs and glands as well as limbs, torso and head. Before providing reflexology it is important to seek advice from a reflexology practitioner. Maps of these points are shown on page 87.

TAC PAC
This is an activity pack based on the idea of tactile play. It is a tactile approach to sensory awareness. It includes resource material in the form of a programme of sensory activities that are matched to musical compositions. Three half-hour tapes with three matching laminated cards provide all the information a parent, carer or teacher would need to set up tactile activities to encourage early communication. The programme uses simple household utensils (e.g. kitchen sponges, wooden spatulas, yellow dusters) and other items (e.g. fans and feathers) to promote sensory activities.

TAC PAC is successfully used in many special schools and pre-school services and it has proven to be a valuable teaching aid for children with complex needs. Address details are listed in the useful addresses section at the back of this book. TAC PAC was devised by Hilary Wainer, Bobbie Storemont and Christine Wright. It comprizes of three half-hour tapes with appropriate tempi and rhythms to accompany specific sensory activities. Pupil are fanned, flicked with little mops, stroked with fur fabric, tapped and rolled with chopsticks, brushed with sponges, drummed with hands, and enjoy other activities, too. Adults encourage children to anticipate sensations and to express their likes and dislikes.

TAC PAC takes approximately an hour to set up and complete. It is important not to rush; to relax and have fun. Always maintain physical contact and keep the person warm, especially if they are undressed in any way. Always start and end with a 'Hello' and 'Finish' song.

The listening programme

This is a sound and auditory stimulation programme, pioneered by Alfred Thomatis, for children from three upwards. It helps balance and restore a person's ability to process sounds across the auditory spectrum, through the careful selection and modification of music, available on audio CDs. The programme entails one to two 15-minute listening sessions a day, five days a week per week, over an eight-week period.

The programme enhances and improves speaking and listening skills, auditory sequential processing, coordination, reading and writing, balance and confidence, attention span and sleep patterns. It has been found beneficial for those who are multiply disabled as well as those with speech problems, dyslexia, dyspraxia, ADHD and autism.

It is available from Advanced Brain Technologies and Unique Sounds and requires high specification headphones and equipment.

Multi-sensory curriculum

Bradley at the Millennium Dome

Bradley meets Goliath

'Multi-sensory education is a formal education course designed to provide full knowledge and understanding of the senses and their application to learning and life. This education should develop sense experience, understanding, perceptions and concepts, so that each learner can reach, stretch and attain their full potential for use throughout their life.'

Longhorn (1992)

Reflexology mapping points

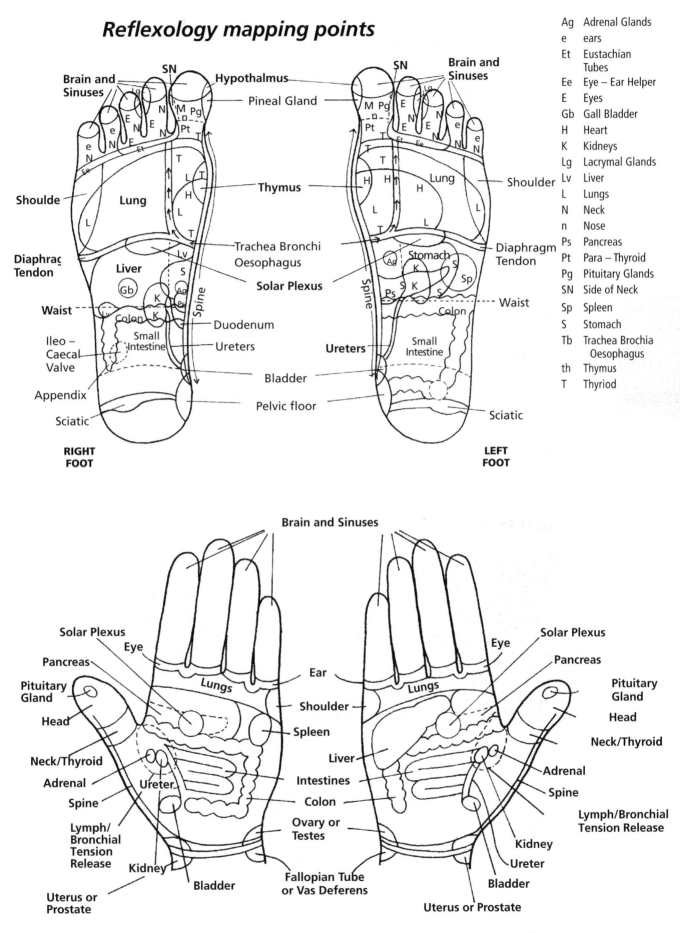

Taken from *The Massage Manual*, Evans, Fransen, and Oxenford (1999)
Copyright of Anness Publishing Ltd.

Children with multiple disabilities require support and guidance to sort out sensory stimuli. The careful planning and teaching of interpreting and organizing sensory information needs to be part of the curriculum for such children. This aspect of learning should not be divorced from their day-to-day tasks and should form the basis of work in all other areas of the curriculum. This approach should be part of a whole-school curriculum and be linked into National Curriculum targets, as well as being incorporated into the writing of Individual Education Programmes.

In planning and facilitating learning, a sensory bank of ideas should be constructed around the learning experience. By analysing and recording the sensory components of the task, learning can be more effectively organized and sorted by the Intervenor and the child. Practical methods of analysis are illustrated below.

Sound: Barn noises, 'clip-clop' of hooves, neighs, rustling of hay, voices with command, a horse chewing and drinking, patting the horse.
Vision: The helper's face, the bobbing up and down of horses, looking down on people, looking between the horse's ears.
Smell: 'Horsey' smells, sawdust, hay, grass, horse food, apples, leather smells, horse's mouth and coat.
Taste: Grass, horse food, the horse's apple, and sometimes the horse.
Touch: A warm horse, a hairy tail and mane, a soft muzzle, patting and stroking the horse, feeling hay and sawdust, water, the helper's touch.
Bodily experience: Getting on and off the horse, controlling the horse, jogging, walking, bobbing up and down, jumping, abrupt stops.

When developing and facilitating a multi-sensory approach, it is important to consider all the different sensations mentioned and not simply focus on the five common senses. This approach concentrates on the development of the senses and of sensory integration. It will implicitly help the child to understand himself and the world around him in an undistorted way. Without this stimulation and awakening of the senses, the world becomes disorganized and confusing.

The child will experience the following sensations:

- choice of shampoo
- smell of shampoo
- feel of warm water spray
- feeling of wet hair
- sensations on the scalp, skin and hair
- smell of hair conditioners
- feel and smell of bubbles and lather
- bodily experience of helping wash hair
- looking at hands and wet hair
- feel of warm towel and
- massage of the scalp.

There are over 50 senses and therefore it is important that we consider all of these in our planning and teaching.

Table of senses

Sight: images, coloure.
Hearing: loud, quiet, moderate, high, low, mid-frequencies.
Smell: good, bad, protective, calming (sedative), stimulating (uplifting), mild, strong.
Touch: pressure, prolonged pressure, warm, hot, cold, vibration, pain, shape, size, wet, dry, rough, smooth, heavy, light, hard, soft.
Taste: salty, bitter, sweet, sour.
Vestibular: fast, slow, acceleration, deceleration, forwards, backwards, sideways, balance, up, down, gravity, motion.
Proprioceptive: spatial, body awareness, coordination, kinaesthetic.

As Longhorn (1992) states:

'A multi-sensory approach aims to use all the child's senses to break through the barrier of a child's handicap and communicate with the child. The multi-sensory experience draws from all the senses, combining their input into an interaction meaningful to the child. The multi-sensory approach encapsulates all the learning experiences of the child, using not only the senses, but the whole range of skills being developed in the overall curriculum.'

4

Key points

- The use and interpretation of sensory information is an essential ingredient in the education of children with multiple disabilities.
- The opportunity to experience a sensory curriculum can naturally be accessed through the National Curriculum and across all areas of school life.
- Understanding the function of the cerebral cortex in relation to a child's individual difficulties is important. This knowledge needs to be incorporated into teaching in order to help the child to make progress and to facilitate good practice.
- When helping children to use sensory information, remember to consider all the senses available to us, not just the five primary senses.
- Problems with sensory integration are common in children with multiple disabilities and those children who have learning difficulties, and these are demonstrated in a variety of ways. Identifying possible sensory difficulties and planning effectively to help children overcome them will bring about more effective teaching and pupil progress.
- It is very important to understand the different ways of improving sensory integration and of reducing tactile defensiveness.
- Interactive massage, aromatherapy and reflexology are available alternatives that have been effective in the education of children with sensory difficulties.

5 | Assessment

Susan is ten years old and attends her local mainstream school with full-time support. She is registered partially sighted and has Bardet-Biedl syndrome. She has a degenerative eye condition and has to be very close to the blackboard to access information. She requires large print and has access to a closed circuit television and a sloping board. Susan is overweight and physically mature for her age. She has a neurological delay in response to questions, with perceptual difficulties. She has a reading age of approximately seven years and enjoys story writing. Susan is supported in class by her peers and special friends, but can aggressively reject them, depending on how she is feeling about her disability. She was encountering many difficulties in her school as a result of insufficient and inappropriate support. This has now been amended and, as a result of this action, she is now fully accessing the curriculum and is much happier. She is very shy and is now overcoming some of her difficulty with poor self-esteem.

'The primary purpose of assessment is to assist in designing intervention strategies.'

Langley (1986)

Assessment is fundamentally concerned with improving the quality of teaching and learning. The term itself is seen to mean different things to different people. However, most would agree that without it, it would be very difficult to plan and facilitate effective teaching and intervention strategies.

It is important to gather as much information as is appropriate before beginning assessment:

- general physical ability and motor impairment
- medical history and medication administered
- global and cognitive functioning
- arousal levels throughout the day
- favoured environmental conditions
- notes on what motivates the child and what he likes.

Arousal levels are very important in the assessment process. There is little point assessing the child when he is drowsy or in a low-arousal state (e.g. following medication or lunch). Any environment the child is placed in needs to be appropriate to the child's individual motivational needs, so that he can act on his environment.

It is important, too, that the child feels at ease during the assessment process. The child will need to be calm and relaxed. Alternatively, the child may need to be galvanized into action.

Also, it is important that the child is placed in a position within his environment that is conducive to learning. Choose a position that minimizes problems of balance, postural control and head control, such as laying the child on his back. The child's position is dependent on the purpose of the assessment (e.g. testing vision or hearing).

Always allow the child sufficient time to respond to and process information during assessment. He will require time to receive and register the input of information, time to interpret this and more time to reply and send messages to relevant parts of the body to produce a response or output.

Decide at the outset of the assessment who should contribute to it. Include the parents and other significant people if possible (e.g. siblings, grandparents), teachers, occupational therapists, physiotherapists, speech therapists and any other relevant professionals (educational psychologist, school nurse/doctor, hospital consultants). You could also include 'fringe significant others', such as lunchtime workers, coach escorts and drivers, and carers.

Purposes of assessment

Assessment identifies those who may require additional support. It can also facilitate a referral to other specialists or special placements. It satisfies legal requirements and provides a tool that can be used to argue for the allocation of resources and funding.

The first basic purpose of assessment is to establish and provide a pupil baseline of ability across the child's global development in order to apply it to their access of the curriculum. It should give objective and factual evidence that has been observed and recorded and can be re-observed by others.

Assessment should be diagnostic, and should identify strengths and abilities, as well as weaknesses and problems. It should lead to a process of evaluating the effectiveness of teaching (which will consider methods, style and content) and will inform those working with the child of progress which has taken place over a prescribed period of time. It will also review the need to evaluate previous interventions and consider their appropriateness or inappropriateness. Assessment should provide a constant review of the child's learning and how progress can be evaluated.

The key to assessment is to record observations specifically, accurately and expediently and facilitate interventions made by colleagues and significant others working with the child. Accurate knowledge of the child's ability will prevent inaccurate assumptions that could lead to low expectations and often underachievement.

Types of assessment

It is very important to select an appropriate assessment tool or package to assess the child. This will need to be matched to the individual

Assessment should be diagnostic and should identify strengths and abilities, as well as weaknesses and problems

Supporting Children

needs of the child, the environment(s), the time available to implement it and the underlying reasons for the assessment taking place. When selecting an appropriate tool, it is important to consider the aspects set out below.

General propositions

Each assessment needs to be clearly defined in advance. The diversity of children with multiple disabilities is such that assessment demands a range of approaches and a high level of individualization. Knowledge of the wide range of published assessment tools available is required, in order to select the most appropriate for each child.

All assessors and assessments carry with them certain assumptions that may blur the judgement of the individual. It is very important to maintain objectivity throughout this process. It must be remembered that with any assessment being undertaken there will be some degree of evaluation concerning the child's received education as well as his ability.

Many assessment tools are based on play (e.g. building a tower of bricks) and are often related to experience. However, some children with multiple disabilities may not have had many of the experiences they are being assessed for, and therefore they will fail. To assume that they have had an experience because of their age or because it would normally be expected is a wrong approach. I once assessed a nine-year-old child who had had no experience of outside play apparatus (roundabouts, etc.) but all those working with this child assumed that he had. They were consequently having difficulties accounting for anxious and disturbing behaviour demonstrated by the child.

Evaluating assessment tools and procedures

When evaluating tools and procedures, the professional needs to consider what demands are being made on the child. These could include visual, auditory, language, intellectual and cooperative behaviour. Also we need to consider what demands are being made on the adult. These demands would include: the knowledge and skills required to operate the tool's procedures; the level of observation skills possessed by the observer; the ability to communicate with the child; and the opportunity of collaboration with other professionals. Time is an important factor in any process. Some tools will need many hours of work and will require a long period of time, over weeks or months. At the outset of assessment, the amount of time that is available should be agreed. The results of the assessment also need to be measured in the light of the length of time available.

The materials and environment available are also important factors. If the assessment requires the use of a sensory room and one is not available, then a different tool should be considered. Assessment tools will need to be age-appropriate. Building a tower of bricks may be an exciting activity for a two- to four-year-old, but to a person who is 15 years old it may not hold the same appeal. Changing it to a tower of video tapes may be more appropriate.

Assessment tools will need to be flexible, and will also need to provide ongoing assessment. Before using a particular assessment test, consider its relevance to the child's future development. Assessment is meaningful only if information gained enables the child, family and educators to make the best use of it.

Current approaches to assessment

There are two main types of assessment approaches: the traditional approach that tends to use a norm-referenced framework; and the more current approaches that tend to be criterion-referenced.

Norm-referenced approach

This approach measures a child's performance, ability and aptitude in relation to his peers' performances. It is a comparative approach that identifies skills that should be achievable by a certain age. The inability to reach these skills in effect raises the question of under-achievement, and may cause the use of the label 'below-average ability' and failure. It compares the development of the individual with the usual sequence of developmental stages.

This approach to assessment uses standardized tests and relies on a score interpretation; it considers 'deviation' from the mean standard score. Sitting down and taking exams (e.g. SATs, GCSEs) is a good example of this type of assessment approach. Reports tend to be summative and will record progress on an occasional or annual basis.

The common types of norm-referenced tests include the following:

● *Psychometric tests* – intelligence tests administered by educational psychologists (e.g. the WISC – language and cognitive test)
● *Reading tests* – Neale, Spar, Salford and McMillan
● *Spelling tests* – Vernon
● *Language tests* – Aston and Reynell.

Criterion-referenced approach

This approach measures achievements and attainment based on what the child can and cannot do. It measures a person's performance relative to a defined criterion. It is more personal and supports individual development and achievement. Pupils are more actively involved in this assessment approach and a wide range of professionals are often included in its deliberations. It is more formative and feeds into continuous assessment.

The nature of this approach is that it provides a checklist of skills and measures a pupil's success by his ability to do a set of tasks. It identifies strengths and weaknesses and can provide a basis for assessing the success of teaching (e.g. proficiency tests such as driving and cycling tests).

Within special education, this approach has been most favoured and most often used, hence the wide variety and choice of tools available on the market. Criterion-referenced tests fall into a number of categories, as listed below:

Developmental/early years:
- Dale's Developmental Guide
- Sheridan's Early Developmental Guide
- Reynel-Zenkin Scale
- Portage
- Oregon.

Language:
- Active Communication Technique (ACT) by Helen Bradley
- Affective Communication Assessment Project (ACAP)
- RL Scale – Broch and League
- Derbyshire
- Distar
- Pre-verbal Communication Schedule
- Pragmatics Profile of Early Communication.

Social and daily living skills:
- Steps to Independence – Best
- Pathways to Independence – Jeffrey and McConkey
- Independent Living – Texas.

General development:
- Gunzburg Progress Assessment Charts
- Vision for Doing
- Parent Assessment of Needs (PAN)
- Kallier-Azusa.

Kallier-Azusa

This is considered the only really effective assessment for multi-sensory-impaired children, and is a comprehensive framework of assessment for individuals. It has two versions, one for children without speech ('G') and one with speech ('H'). It bases its observations over a two-week period with at least two people, as part of a team approach to assessment. It gives a score in each developmental/curriculum area and has a detailed holistic approach to the child. However, it does unfortunately take a very long time to complete.

Gunzberg progress assessment charts

Gunzberg (1974) devised a series of progress assessment charts (PAC) which focused on the social and personal development of children with special needs. They included self-help skills, communication, socialization, and personal autonomy (which he referred to as 'occupation'). All activities led to personal independence and records were scored on a pie chart matrix, which clearly identified strengths and weaknesses at a quick glance. These charts were very popular many years ago because of the way information was recorded and because of its emphasis on acquiring independence skills.

Vision for doing

This is a tool for assessing functional vision of learners who are multiple disabled, devised by Aitken and Buultjens (1992). It provides a series of charts that include the assessment of vision, the senses, mobility and use of computers and switches. This is a very useful tool; however, it tends to be used in bits rather than as a whole because of its format and the time it takes to complete.

Observation skills

It is crucial for professionals to develop good observation skills. Observation can be either intentional or accidental. Many times, when someone is observing something specific, they may accidentally discover something else they did not expect. The main purpose of observation is to make an accurate record of behaviour; that is, to make a record of observations with which someone else would agree. Observation needs to be objective, unbiased and non-inferential.

We need to observe in order to find out, first hand the full range of behaviour likely to be shown by a child. We may want to identify unusual behaviour or find out more about a particular aspect of behaviour.

Observation schedules need to be focused and specific. They cannot record everything. They need to be represented numerically and allow for systematic comparisons. They need to be accurate and reliable and economical with time.

A number of questions need to be asked when devising an observation schedule:

- Is this activity enjoyable and meaningful to the child?
- Does it meet a need for the child?
- Are expressed wishes acknowledged and respected?
- Is the activity structured so that expectations are assessable?
- Is the adult willing to 'change tack' and to follow the child's lead?
- Is the child offered genuine choices?
- Does the adult communicate her intentions to the child?
- Is it clear to the child when a choice is offered?
- Is the child able to control the pace of the activity, curtail or prolong actions and initiate actions?
- Is the child handled with respect and affection?
- Does the adult give undivided attention to the child?

- Does communication take place at a level appropriate to the child and in a mode appropriate to that child?
- Are indications of mood or opinion respected?
- Is difficult behaviour analysed with communication in mind?

Observation schedules

There are many ways of making accurate observations. The main ways are listed below.

Diary descriptions

These are very general comments recorded in the child's file, and cover progress, problems and developmental changes. These records need to be timed and dated.

Specimen descriptions

These are similar to diary descriptions, but concentrate more on the detail of single episodes of behaviour, recording antecedents and contingencies (before and after the event). This is often referred to as ABC (Antecedent, Behaviour and Contingencies) charts (see page 99 for photocopiable chart).

Time sampling

Time sampling records selected aspects of behaviour within specified intervals of time. This method is usually used with a fixed interval sampling sheet, which measures the frequency of the behaviour or activity being exhibited. Used in conjunction with this means of recording observations are two tools: a tally counter and a teacher prompt. A tally counter is very useful and is more versatile and expedient than a record sheet. A teacher prompt is another useful tool. The function of this device is that every time the bleep sounds or alarm is emitted, the teacher records the behaviour, either using the tally counter or record sheet. At the end of the fixed period, a record of incidents can be totalled (see page 100 for photocopiable chart).

Event sampling

This involves recording in detail each instance of a particular behaviour or task and may be used in conjunction with the ABC chart. It considers the time of the event, whether the child was on- or off-task and records who was involved with the child at the time (see page 101 for photocopiable chart).

Rating scales

This is a direct observation without distraction, where the observer both judges and observes behaviour and it is then scored.

Longitudinal observations or studies

This is when the child is assessed at the beginning of a programme, during the programme and at the end. Judgments and tasks are recorded on an ongoing basis.

Interviewing

Interviewing is another informative and popular way of gathering useful information to assess learning and behaviour. This is a mechanism for the teacher and significant others to ask the pupils questions. It can be facilitated through an interview or a questionnaire or a combination of both.

Interviewing can be either directive or non-directive. In directive questioning, questions tend to be of a closed nature, less personal and friendly, and tend to be more formal. A directive interview is only as good as the questions being asked, and can often leave many other questions unanswered. With a non-directive interviewing technique, the whole situation is more open and flexible, more personal and less cold in its approach. It incorporates the use of a series of open questions that can be extended or curtailed according to what sort of information is needed. It involves the use of 'door openers' (e.g. 'that's interesting', 'tell me more', 'uh-hmm'), brief expectant pauses, neutral requests, echoing the interviewee's responses, reflecting the person's feelings, paraphrasing sections of the interview to check information, and using physical attending behaviour (e.g. eye contact, relaxed sitting position, not crossing your arms).

Interviewing pupils with multiple disabilities presents many difficulties, but the results of listening to their replies and respecting their decisions can have amazing results and lead to many solutions.

Questionnaires

Questionnaires use a combination of open and closed questions and have the advantage of providing a formal record of answers to questions, as well as being a carefully constructed series of questions that can be generally distributed to all potential customers. The disadvantage is that not all people like to respond in a detailed manner and may not reveal all, if the question is not directive enough. Questionnaires tend to be time consuming and impersonal, and, again, they are only as good as the questions being asked.

Task analysis

This is a behavioural approach to simplifying tasks that would be otherwise complicated. It breaks down tasks into smaller sequential steps which lead to the final behaviour. Each step needs to be mastered and achieved before moving on to the next step. Each step can be rewarded on its completion. If the steps are too large, the pupil has less chance of success and reward, and they may fail. This technique involves making clear statements of objectives and encourages individualization. There are four commonly used methods in task analysis.

Chaining

Forward chaining teaches the steps of a task in their naturally occurring order. In backward chaining, the steps of each task are taught in reverse order, teaching the last steps first. Before a task can

The ABC chart

Name of pupil

Date	Time	Antecenent	Behaviour	Contingencies

5

Fixed interval sampling

Pupil		Class		No. in class		Observer		Date

Activity							Setting	

Class Behaviour Rating -2 -1 0 +1 +2

	00	15	30	45	00	15	30	45	00	15	30	45	(1) On Task	(2) Talking	(3) Looking	(4) Physical	(5) Movement	(6) Fidgeting	(7) Noise	(8) Other

Event sampling chart

Name of pupil ....

Date ....   Place ....

Engaged	Inappropriate	Staff attention	Doing nothing
✔1 = Person	✗ = Target	= Circled	= O
✔2 = Object	✗O = Other	(✗)	
✔3 = Per + Obj			

Description of target behaviour:

Time	✔ O ✗	Details	Time	✔ O ✗	Details	Summary	

5

be taught using this approach, the steps required to teach it need to be accurately broken down into small steps. The next stage is to identify where the child is on that continuum and then to decide whether to use a forward or backward chaining approach.

This method is commonly used for teaching daily living skills (e.g. washing, dressing, drinking, eating, etc.). However, the approach of breaking tasks down into smaller, more achievable steps has now become more widely used across all areas of the curriculum and is seen as good teaching practice.

Shaping

Shaping is a technique where the child is expected to carry out the same complete action for each of the stages, but the teaching materials are graded, in order to make the task progressively more demanding. This approach is particularly useful for hand-eye coordination or fine-motor control.

A commonly encountered example is the skill of threading a needle, in which the child is taken from the first step, involving a needle with a large-sized hole to be threaded with string, though to the final stage, using a conventional darning needle or a normal sewing needle with finer thread.

Errorless discrimination learning

This method is not so frequently used. As the title implies, the tasks are made as 'foolproof' as possible. The level of difficulty is controlled in two ways:

● Steps which gradually increase the number of choices available, from a first step in which only 'correct' objects are presented, up to a final stage in which the number of choices mirror those present in everyday life.

● Steps which gradually make it harder to distinguish between the correct items and the wrong ones.

Fading

Fading involves the gradual reduction of prompts or supportive cues. An illustration of its use is in writing and forming letters and numerals as seen below.

Prompts are the various ways of supporting children to complete tasks. They include physical guidance and touch, verbal instructions and interpretation, and effective use of adaptive equipment. Prompts are important in enabling children to complete tasks; however, the system of the reduction of prompts is equally as important. When a system of prompts is introduced, a grading system of prompt reduction will also be required.

Trace over   Independent use

Baselines

A baseline assessment is the key to providing good quality education to children with multiple disabilities. It informs parents, professionals and national bodies of children's abilities and inabilities, and their strengths and weaknesses. It is essential that accurate baselines are established for children. However, this becomes difficult if there is not an appropriate assessment tool available.

There are five stages involved in establishing a child's baseline:

1 Assess the child on the target skill.
2 Determine which steps he can perform within the task.
3 Set out the prompts which are needed for those steps.
4 Consider prompt reduction.
5 Systematically record progress.

'P' Scales

In 1997, the Qualifications and Curriculum Authority (QCA) published the Baseline Assessment Scales for Children with Special Educational Needs. However, this document failed to include a large number of pupils with multiple disability, leaving them without a national baseline assessment.

The 'P' Scale grew out of this document, and attempts to address those pupils who are working towards Level 1 of the National Curriculum. The scale scores attainment according to performance points, under the headings of literacy, mathematics and personal and social development. Previously there was no recognized tool to accompany the National Curriculum assessment procedure and many children with multiple disabilities received a score of zero or the statement 'Working towards Level One'.

Achieving a score on a National Baseline Guide is recognition of the abilities of multiple disabled children. It shows that they are interactive communicators who need to be treated with greater respect and dignity as learners.

In 2001, QCA published a document of a series of eight 'P' (Pupil Performance) levels across 13 National Curriculum subjects, with three generic levels, applicable for children of all ages.

Since then a number of companies have further developed the use and recording of 'P' Levels and are being used as baseline assessment guides. They include Equals, PIVATS and B Squared. All three systems inform target setting, show pupil progression and are available on CD to be used digitally. It is important, however, that none of these systems become the programme for the child. They should be used as a guide towards a holistic learning programme and for progression and national assessment.

Key points
- Gather as much information about the child as possible from those people who know him best.
- Identify the purpose of the assessment from its outset.
- Decide on an appropriate tool to match the needs of the child and the purpose of the assessment.
- Decide on the type of observation schedule to be used.
- Identify what motivates the child from observation and through discussions with those who know the child.
- Allow the child additional time to process information before requesting more information.
- Ascertain the child's baseline before establishing a teaching programme and allocating staff and resources.

6 | Access to appropriate environments

Mandy is five years old and has quadriplegic cerebral palsy. She suffers from epilepsy and has gastroesophagal reflux. She has a developmental delay with only light perception. Mandy attends a mainstream school with a resourced provision for children who have complex needs. She communicates her needs through a range of sounds, laughs and cries, and quietens to familiar friendly voices. She has poor head control and is unable to weight-bear. Mandy enjoys mouthing objects and prefers to operate within her own internal world. She loves playing on the resonance board and proactively initiates activities using this equipment. When she uses vibro-tactile equipment she involves herself in activities outside her own world. Mandy enjoys working alongside her peers, although she is still a child locked in her own world. Inclusion is motivating her to be part of this world, and her friends very much want this.

'The child should feel that he is not at the mercy of his environment, but that he is able to control it and to influence it.'

Van Dijk (1966)

In this chapter, two aspects of appropriate environments for children with multiple disabilities will be considered. The first is the nature of the school building and the different requirements of each location. This section is particularly useful when designing and modifying a mainstream school and would also be useful in considering whether existing schools are inclusive schools or not. The second is the importance of reactive environments and their role in facilitating education for children who are multiple disabled.

The school building

There are a number of key features that should be incorporated in the design of buildings to meet the access needs of children with multiple disabilities.

A good design is one which enables children to gain access to and move around within a building freely, independently, safely and with peace of mind. The design should enhance both the functional efficiency and the aesthetic appeal of the premises for all users. It needs to enhance the use of the child's sensory system to provide a wide variety of clues about the environment.

Buildings on one level are advantageous. However, if the school has a number of floors, this may not be problematic if the layout on each level is consistent with the others and if a stair lift is available.

External approach

The external approach to the school should be flat and level where possible. If a change of level is unavoidable, a ramp conforming to the gradient and length set out in Building Regs Part M 1992 should be provided. Steps should also be provided with appropriate and uniform tread and riser, colour contrasted or highlighted nosing on every step, and a handrail on both sides. Any ornamentation or decoration on the approach should be positioned in such a way that it does not constitute an obstacle or hazard, and is clearly visible during daylight and hours of darkness.

Entrance

The main entrance to the premises should be clearly visible and distinguishable from the rest of the front of the building. It should be flat and level. Particular care should be exercised when designing doors. Rotating doors should be avoided. Automatic sliding doors are suitable. The doors should be in pairs with each half measuring at least 800mm wide. The threshold should be nominally flush with a weatherbar a maximum height of 15mm.

A tactile surface can help in finding the position of a doorway, as can the use of signs, lighting and audible tones/beacons. Doors should be fitted with self-closing mechanisms. Both doors should be free to open if they are in pairs. The doors and adjacent panels may be glazed. It is an important safety feature to ensure that the glazed panels should be highlighted with some decorative feature at approximately a child's eye level. If it is necessary to provide a door mat inside the entrance, it should be recessed, flush with the surrounding floor.

Careful consideration should be given to the level of lighting immediately inside the entrance doors. Moving from bright sunlight into the dark interior of a building can be distressing. This situation can be avoided by providing a dimmer switch to adjust lighting conditions or moderately powered lighting.

Signs

● *Visibility*: It is important that a sign, which is there solely to give information, is highly visible and in a prominent position. The sign should not be surrounded by other items such as advertising material which will distract attention from the sign.

- *Clarity*: Both the design and the message must be clear. Complicated messages and fussy designs are difficult to read and understand.
- *Position*: Signs need to be positioned at the height of the intended user. If they are for children to read then they need to be at a realistic height for them to access the information.
- *Lighting*: Care should be taken to ensure that a sign is adequately lit during hours of darkness. Lights should be positioned away from the sign and shielded so that they do not cause glare.
- *Style*: The lettering on a sign should be clear and simple. A good font is Helvetica Bold, in lower case lettering. Each letter should stand alone and should not be linked to the following letter. The use of italics is to be avoided.
- *Colour*: Signs should use a strong background colour with light lettering. Good background colours are black, dark blue, dark green and dark red. Good colours for lettering are bright white or yellow.

Classroom

The classroom layout should be simple enabling pupils to be independent, and feel at ease in the room. There should be sufficient space for children to be able to access all areas without moving objects or pupils. There should be a consistent layout of furniture that is predictable and not liable to change without warning. Furniture should not have sharp edges and or be made of material (e.g. iron) that would inflict bodily damage if it was struck by a child. Low-level objects can be dangerous if they cannot be predicted. Height adjustable tables are advisable.

Doors need to have closures. This reduces sudden noises of banging doors and prevents them remaining open. Doors will also need to be wide enough for wheelchair access.

Floors need to be clear and uncluttered in areas where children may be at risk from falling over objects or toys. Floor covering should be firmly fixed to the floor and not have tears or be curling up as this could cause an accident.

Walls and displays should not have sharp edges or protruding staples. Leads and trailing wires from electrical appliances should not run across the floor. They should either be avoided or be covered by a non-slip mat. There should be storage areas for mobility equipment.

Lighting should be uniform, and fluorescent lighting is preferable. The lighting should be housed within diffused and reflective fittings providing a minimum 450 to 600 lux level. Light fittings should be of a high-frequency nature in order to be flicker-free. Fluorescent tubes need to be white with daylight simulation if possible. Dimmer switches are useful to gain greater control of lighting conditions. Blinds may need to be installed where bright daylight and glare are a problem.

Walls and doors should be appropriately coloured and contrasted. Special teaching areas need to be marked (e.g. home/book corner) by the use of different colours, flooring, etc. Cupboards, shelves and

6

A classroom environment checklist

(Rikhye, Gothelf, and Appell – 1989)

Tick – Yes or No.	Yes	No
1. Would you want your relative to spend the day in this classroom?	☐	☐
2. Is the classroom cheerful and pleasant?	☐	☐
3. Are the equipment, decor, furniture and wall displays age appropriate?	☐	☐
4. Is the environment safe?	☐	☐
5. Are work areas organized, neat, labelled and accessible?	☐	☐
6. Is the classroom organized to allow privacy during change of clothing?	☐	☐
7. Is there an appropriate level of sensory stimulation in the classroom?	☐	☐
8. Is the furniture the correct size for each pupil?	☐	☐
9. Does each pupil have and use appropriate adaptive equipment?	☐	☐
10. Is each pupil's equipment in good working order?	☐	☐
11. Are lighting levels sufficient and are light sources individualized and adjustable?	☐	☐
12. Does the classroom have adequate sound-dampening?	☐	☐
13. Does the organization of the room promote orientation and independent mobility?	☐	☐
14. Does the organization of the room promote anticipation of classroom activities?	☐	☐
15. Are pupils' belongings tactually or visually identified?	☐	☐
16. Is the class timetable displayed?	☐	☐
17. Are IEPs displayed?	☐	☐
18. Is the means of recording pupil progress in view?	☐	☐
19. Are photographs and descriptions of prescribed positions for pupils who have physical impairments displayed?	☐	☐
20. Would you want your relative to spend the day in this classroom?	☐	☐

6

materials should be clearly labelled in large print or, alternatively, by using either a colour or shape or tactile code. Displays should be mounted in a way that enables all children to appreciate them. Print, drawings or tactile code should be at hand level or just above so they can be easily read with the fingers.

A good supply of power points should be available. Floor-mounted power points would be useful as this would reduce trailing leads. These should be recessed and positioned suitably to comply with desk and table arrangements. Separate teaching areas should also be available for individual teaching.

Reception area

This should be well lit and colour or tone contrasting should be used to clearly identify the reception desk, entrance to toilets and other facilities. High-gloss floor finishes which reflect light should be avoided. Attention should be paid to the acoustics in this area as a high level of noise is both confusing and distressing. Carpeting is a more suitable floor covering. Direction signs, displays and notices should be carefully positioned and carefully illuminated with matt finish so that they do not reflect light. A tactile map could be provided, showing the general layout of the school. A classroom environment checklist has been provided on page 108 in order to help professionals to think more about their current school environment. Questions 1 and 20 are the same; however, your answers may be different as a result of your previous answers.

Stairs

Stairs and steps should be well and evenly illuminated. The treads and risers should be uniform. Each step should be covered with a highlighted or coloured nosing which clearly contrasts with the rest of the flooring. Bands of dark colour on the edge of stair treads, are particularly beneficial. A yellow line 10cm wide in the middle of the stairs can demark up and down walking areas.

A tactile warning strip could be provided at the top and bottom of a flight of stairs. There should be a continuous handrail on both sides. A handrail should extend across landing areas. It should have a ridge or other feature which indicates the approach to the first or last step. The handrail should be of a clearly contrasting colour. The floor number should be clearly indicated by a sign at the top and bottom of the staircase or by the use of tactile markings or objects of reference.

Stair entrances/exits and landings should be well lit. Lighting is especially important around bends. Switches will need to be located on the left side of the person at the bottom/top of stairways and networked to each other. They should be at a consistent height and should be predictably located. Switch fittings should be well contrasted to the wall colour (not white unless the walls are dark).

Corridors

Corridors should be wide enough to allow convenient and safe passage for those in a wheelchair or accompanied by sighted escorts. Corridors

6

should be as straight as possible and changes of direction should be at a right angle. Corridor walls should be unobstructed uncluttered, and any essential fittings should be recessed. Good quality lighting is very important to ensure safety and provide visual and sensory information. Painted lines 10cm wide may be painted on the floor leading pupils to important areas (i.e. library, reception). If external windows are fitted at the end of a corridor they should be fitted with curtains or blinds to prevent glare and to clearly indicate the end of a corridor.

Doors

Any doors should swing back flush to the wall and be capable of being opened easily and without applying too much pressure. If the doors are glazed, they must carry some clearly visible identifications at a child's eye level. The door frame and door furnishing should be clearly distinct in colour from the surrounding areas. Doors should not be fitted close to steps. Colour contrasting should be used to clearly distinguish the floor from the walls of the corridor. Objects of reference can be placed  on doors to give further information. All staff and pupils need to be aware of safety issues and keep doors closed.

Lighting

Lighting should be reasonably uniform and pools of lighting and dark should be avoided. Fluorescent tube lighting is considered to be the best as it provides more light and is cheapest. The lighting should be housed within diffused and reflective fittings providing a minimum 250 lux level. Light fittings should be of a high-frequency nature in order to be flicker-free. Fluorescent tubes need to be white with daylight simulation. Blinds may need to be installed where bright daylight and glare are a problem. Entrances to key areas (e.g. hall and dining room) require additional lighting to highlight their location and to help children negotiate a potential hazard.

Toilets

Lighting should be adequate and light fittings, floors and other surfaces should be designed not to cause glare. Colour and texture contrasting should be used to clearly identify doors, door furniture, washbasins, taps, etc. The entrance to the toilet should be indicated by a tactile floor surface, by clearly contrasting colour entrance doors, and by the provision of a tactile sign or object of reference on the door or on the adjacent wall.

6

Hall/Dining room

Entrance and exit doors should be clearly indicated and fitted with self-closing devices. The general layout of tables and chairs should be in a regular pattern, not at random, with sufficient gangway space. Tables and chairs should be in a colour which clearly contrasts with the floor finish. Lighting should be sufficient and pools of light and dark should again be avoided. Carrying trays and crockery should ideally be in colours which clearly contrast with each other and also with the surface of the table.

Fire exits/Escapes

Fire exits should be clearly marked by colour-contrasting doors and have illuminated signs above. Additional lighting needs to be placed at these points to highlight their location. In the event of a fire or power failure, emergency illuminating lighting above each fire exit should be provided and this should be supplemented with an audible beacon saying 'Fire exit this way'. Floor lighting may be helpful for those who are deafblind. Tactile signs should be used to indicate exits.

Any external fire exits must be provided with a handrail on both sides which should be continuous and painted white or yellow. Any changes in step elevation should be clearly indicated by a marker on the handrails.

Colour and tone contrast

Careful selection of colours will assist in a number of ways. A consistent choice of colours will help locate those items that occur regularly, such as doors. Some colour coding may be possible to differentiate, for example, the toilet doors from classroom doors. Surfaces should incorporate the use of strong colour contrasts which are shown clearly against light matt areas and dark coloured areas. Walls should be painted in light, matt colours. Doors and door frames should be painted in strong colours (e.g. yellow). Doors could be a different colour from the door frame. White light switches should be contrasted with a pale-cloured wall and have a yellow band around them. The door handle should be distinctive from the door colour (e.g. do not have a silver handle and a white door).

Edges between walls and floors, ceilings and walls need to be distinctive, using pale and matt colours. Coloured strips on glass panels are required

6

on doors. The effectiveness of colour and tone contrasting can be tested by taking a black and white photograph of the relevant area.

Textural contrast and tactile clues

Foot clues for doors, key areas, stairs and other hazard zones are beneficial. This can be done by using a textured mat recessed into the floor or carpet or rubberized, textured surfacing. Tactile clues are very useful for trailing and can include textured strips along the wall or corridor, or textured material or objects of reference to denote specific areas, rooms or floors.

Tactile markers and objects of reference, at key points may also give additional information. Furniture and decorative objects (e.g. statues, waterfalls) could be available in the school to provide useful landmarks for the child.

Acoustic conditions

The sound level in the school and classroom should be low to enable sound cues to be picked up easily. An echoey environment should be avoided. Hard surfaces against which objects clatter are of no use. Furniture should have rubber feet. Blinds, double glazing, special acoustic panels, carpets and rubberized floors help to keep background noise low, allowing meaningful sounds to be more audible to the child. Adults need to be aware of the existence in some rooms of 'acoustic deadspots', areas in the room where sound is not clearly audible.

Outside areas

It is important that all paths and entrances be well lit. Care and consideration of colour and tone contrast, textural contrast and tactile clues and signage are also key elements in providing safe and independent environments. A yellow line 10cm wide may be painted on the path surface leading to and from key areas as another useful indicator. Outside play areas need surfaces that are even and firm. A non-reflective and non-slip surface such as a playscread surface is beneficial and safe.

Playground apparatus should be colour contrasted with the floor as this will provide good visual clues, as well as support to aid depth perception. Brightly coloured equipment will also look aesthetically appealing and will motivate children to use and enjoy it.

Equipment storage areas

Storage facilities for large equipment should be spread around the building and not put in one place. This will make equipment more accessible and will avoid further clutter. Be careful that these stores do not lead to more obstructions. Equipment should not be left in corridors for safety reasons and space should be designed to accommodate this.

Hygiene room

Hygiene rooms include a wide range of furniture and equipment. A basin with lever taps and space for the adult to wash the pupil's hands is helpful. A small/large toilet with height adjustable grab rails is required. If a shower is to be installed, a low sloped shower tray for wheelchair accessibility is adviseable. A mobile hoist or H-frame is required to transfer pupils. Additional equipment could include a washing machine for soiled clothes and an electric height adjustable changing bed with drop-down sides.

Sensory gardens

A sensory garden is an asset to an outside environment. A careful layout of plants will facilitate a very pleasurable experience, and the plants can be used within the school for aromatherapy. All those listed below are available from a good garden centre. Each require fertile soil and sunlight. When crushed or touched will they each emit the required scent. The importance of a sensory garden is that it can be effectively used in calming children who are overactive by placing them in the appropriate section. The reverse is true, in that children who are very passive and need to be aroused and more alert, can be placed in the uplifting section. Sensory gardens are not flower arrangement areas where flowers are chosen for their beauty. However, other flowers can be incorporated into the design for this effect.

Sensory garden herbs

Calming/Relaxing	Calming/Uplifting	Uplifting/Alertness
Lavender	Parsley	Bergamot
Camomile	Thyme	Rosemary
Lemon Balm	Lovage	Mint
Lemon Verbena		Rose
		Geranium
		Mock Orange
		Elder
		Fennel
		Chives
		Curry
		Chervil

- *Mock Orange* (*Philadelphus*) – Deciduous shrubs that grow up to 2m high with white flowers.
- *Geranium* (scented leaf) – Plant with different coloured flowers and are removed in winter.
- *Parsley* – Low-growing perennial plant with white flowers.
- *Lovage* – Perennial plant that grows up to 2m high with yellow or green flowers. Known as the 'giant' of the herb world.

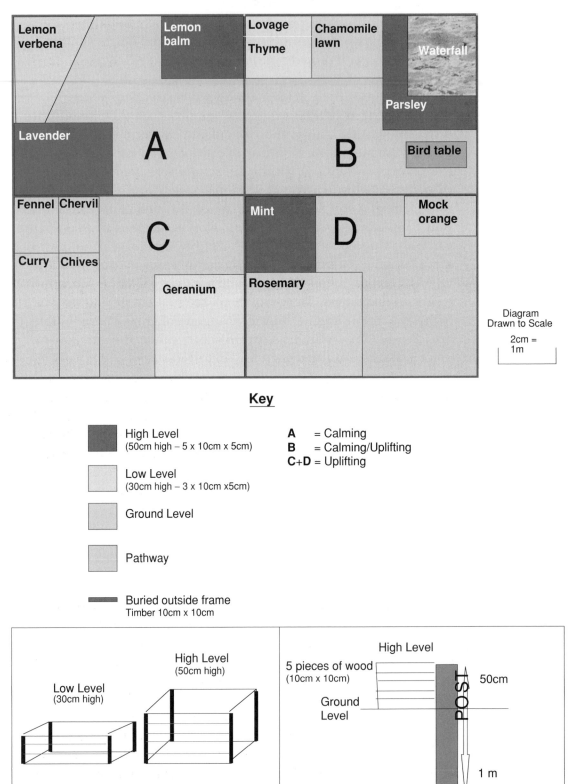

Sensory Garden
(8m x 6m)

Lemon verbena

Lemon balm

Lovage
Thyme

Chamomile lawn

Waterfall

Parsley

Lavender

A

B

Bird table

Fennel | Chervil

C

Mint

D

Mock orange

Curry | Chives

Geranium

Rosemary

Diagram
Drawn to Scale

2cm =
1m

Key

High Level
(50cm high – 5 x 10cm x 5cm)

Low Level
(30cm high – 3 x 10cm x5cm)

Ground Level

Pathway

Buried outside frame
Timber 10cm x 10cm

A = Calming
B = Calming/Uplifting
C+**D** = Uplifting

Low Level
(30cm high)

High Level
(50cm high)

High Level

5 pieces of wood
(10cm x 10cm)

POST

50cm

Ground
Level

1 m

10cm x 10cm

- *Camomile* – Creeping low-growing perennial with white and yellow flowers.
- *Bergamot* – Perennial plant growing up to 60cm with scarlet flowers.
- *Elder* (*Sambucus*) – Tree with white blossom followed by purple berries.
- *Rosemary* – Evergreen shrub of up to 2m high with blue flowers.
- *Thyme* – Evergreen small shrub with pink flowers.
- *Mint* (garden mint) – Low-growing perennial plant with blue flowers. Place in pots to avoid undue spreading.
- *Lemon Verbena* – Deciduous shrub growing up to 5m with mauve flowers.
- *Lemon Balm* – Shrub growing up to 60cm high with white flowers.
- *Lavender* – Shrub growing up to 1m high with purple flowers.
- *Curry* – Perennial plant growing up to 1m with bright yellow flowers.
- *Chives* – Perennial vegetable with purple flowers.
- *Fennel* – Perennial plant growing up to 2m with yellow flowers.
- *Chervil* – Low-growing perennial with white flowers (similar smell to fennel).
- *Chamomile Lawn* – This is grass sown with chamomile seeds. When walked on will emit a strong smell. The previous diagram provides a scaled drawing of a possible layout for a sensory garden.

The sensory garden plan on page 115 identifies a possible design layout. Using the ideas in this plan will enable the reader to build a sensory garden. It is important that it is wheelchair accessible and that children can move around the garden with adequate space and mobility. It is also important that the flowers are arranged at different levels (ground, low and high) for accessibility and aesthetic shape. The timber should be treated appropriately for outside use and be secured safely. A sensory garden can be further enhanced by the use of hanging wind chimes and by providing outside seating.

Reactive Environments

Due to a lack of awareness of the world, children who are multiple disabled often require the use of reactive environments to promote communication, cause and effect, mobility and general learning. Using reactive environments is a very important tool in helping children to access the environments and to understand them.

Nielsen (1992) views these children as sensory deprived and says that they have no way of learning that interesting sounds relate to any other sensory experience, let alone physical objects, so the desire to reach out and explore does not develop. Many children become passive listeners, often becoming very still in order to hear better, but with no understanding of what they hear. They develop a sense of learnt passive helplessness.

Reactive environments provide the opportunity to counteract this sense of learnt helplessness or sensory deprivation. They encourage the child to explore and to initiate movement and so develop the concept of self as an active 'doer'. They increase deliberate movements and provide an environment in which children can achieve a frame of reference concerning objects in relation to each other and to themselves.

These environments include:

- little rooms
- resonance boards
- acoustic bells
- environmental platforms
- therapy balls
- multi-sensory rooms (and associated equipment)
- switch technology
- vibro-tactile equipment
- mobiles
- suspended rooms.

Schools will need to provide opportunities and space for these environments and understand how they are used to promote communication, learning and sensory stimulation.

Little rooms

Nielsen (1992) developed the idea of the 'little room' when working with visually impaired young children with multiple disabilities. A little room is a three-sided box with a lid, turned on its side, with objects suspended on elastic strands from its lid.

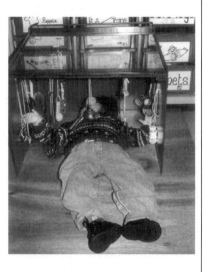

Little rooms provide children with the ability to learn about small environments before dealing with the whole world. This makes them feel more safe and secure and reduces spatial fears and external distraction.

They give a stable environment where it is easy to replicate the exact layout each time it is used with a particular child. Objects can remain fixed and predictable and provide opportunities for developing a directed reach and an alternating gaze. They allow opportunities for the child to explore and discover at his own pace. They encourage individual and independent play movement and vocalization.

Children can be placed inside the Little Room, either by prone lying or sitting. Alternatively, they can be placed outside, either lying on their side or sitting looking in.

Teaching points

- Do not direct the child's hands.
- Do not overload the child with too many objects.
- Carefully consider the objects you do place in the Little Room: use sound-making toys/objects, visually attractive toys/objects and tactile objects.
- Remember to make sure that the objects are securely fastened and safe.
- Give the child plenty of time and remember that he may need periods of rest in between periods of activity.
- Observe the child and record his progress.
- Have the availability to control lighting. This can be achieved through using flaps and panels.
- The inter-change of panels (i.e. dark or reflective or bright) needs to be available to control lighting, mood and change of purpose.
- The size needs to be comfortable and adjustable to the user.
- The room needs to be adaptable to meet the varying needs of a number of pupils.
- There should be an option of changing the length of the mobile strands, so that objects can rest on those children who are very passive (any body movement will result in the movement of objects) and be higher up for those who are developing reaching skills.

Little Rooms can be cheaply provided with a little imagination and thought. Suggestions include the use of containers (e.g. large ice-cream containers), large cardboard boxes, tables covered with sheeting or blankets and tents.

Professionally made Little Rooms are readily available, such as the BeeActive Box by Suffolk Playworks.

Resonance boards

This is another idea originating from Lilli Nielsen. A Resonance Board is a board that children sit or lie on and receive vibratory information which increases their awareness or interest in the activity and the environment they are in.

When a child is laid on the Resonance Board with a variety of objects around him, small movements that he makes will cause sounds to be magnified and the resulting vibrations can be felt. This may help to improve the understanding of a relationship between movement, sound and touch. This, in turn, increases awareness of position of the limbs.

When using the Resonance Board with a child for the first time, you may want to dampen the resonance of the board by placing a pillow or blanket under his head, whilst he is lying down, until he

Little Rooms provide children with the ability to learn about small environments before dealing with the whole world

6

is used to it. A child can also sit next to the board with bare feet while being held by an adult. Children can lie or sit.

Using the board in the way described provides a 'reactive environment' where a child has the opportunity for independent interaction with his environment. Movements the child makes result in immediate sound, movement and vibration from the toy, through the board. The child should be allowed to interact at his own pace without adult intervention, but he should always be supervised to ensure the child's safety and monitor progress.

The Resonance Board can also be used for an adult to interact with the child. Adults can use the Resonance Board to call the child by his name using their own voice, directing their voice to the board, so that it can be acoustically reflected. The adult can then use her hands to tap out single beats, progressing to three or four repeated patterns, waiting for the child to make a reciprocal response. The child quite often begins to lead these kinds of activities, if he is allowed to by the adult. These tasks will provide the child with opportunities to respond, anticipate, turn-take or ask for more.

Use of the board with some children will provide opportunities to develop an understanding of space by learning about the limited space of the board and the space beyond it.

Resonance Boards can be used for group activities. The class can sit around the perimeter of the board and follow a number of activities using their voices or hands to tap out rhythms. It is more stimulating if children place their bare feet on the Resonance Board.

When considering children who are tactile defensive, it is advisable for the adult to use real objects rather than their voice or hands, as these children may see these as less threatening. Not only can a white drum beater be used for tapping out rhythms, it can also be used to encourage visual tracking skills.

Equipment to use on the board depends upon personal preferences.

The following may be useful:

● your own voice and hands
● wind-up music boxes

- rocking toys with a chime
- plastic/metal Slinkies
- spinning tops
- bells (either on a bracelet around their feet or wrist or with a handle)
- drum beater
- chains of various lengths and weights
- bunches of metal keys
- tape recorder with music
- rubber mats can create a friction-like stimulation effect.

The Resonance Board is often used in conjunction with the Little Room and this combination provides an even more reactive environment. An environmental platform can also be turned upside down and used as a Resonance Board.

Teaching Stages for a Resonance Board

1 For the child to kneel or sit beside the board resting their hands on the board. The adult should then bang the board with their hand or beater and encourage the child to return the banging message.

2 Sit the child on the floor next to the board and place their feet on the board (with and without their socks on). The adult should then use a beater or their hands to make the vibrations. A tape recorder playing music with a strong beat could be used.

3 Sit the child on the board with their legs apart, playing freely with appropriate equipment (as above). The adult can sit alongside the child following similar activities as above.

4 The child can be placed on all fours and continue to enjoy the activities played.

5 The child can lie on his front.

6 Lay the child on his back, head supported by a cushion. This will dampen the sound and resonance value.

7 Lay the child on his back, head unsupported.

It is important that these stages are observed to avoid tactile defensivenes and aversion to this environment. Using the board in an incorrect manner can create unnecessary anxiety and fear. The maximum body resonance value is to be found in Stage 7. It may be helpful for the adult to experience each of these stages for himself, to fully appreciate their differences.

Making a Resonance Board

A possible design that provides maximum resonance is made from a board 120cm square. The following materials are required for this design: one piece of marine plywood (4mm to 8mm thick) 120cm square; four pieces of plywood 2.5cm × 2.5cm (each 175cms long); wood glue; short nails or screws; and a tin of furniture wax. The four pieces are glued and nailed around the underside edges of the piece of plywood, making certain that the nails are hammered well in to leave the plywood surface safe. Then the upper surface of the plywood needs to be made very smooth with sandpaper. The final step is to apply at least two coats of funiture wax to the plywood with a duster so the finished surface is smooth and easy to clean. The resonance value will also improve using wax rather than varnish. A baby-size board can be made which is more portable (90cm square), though it does not resonate as well as the larger one. Maintenance needs depend on the amount of use, although it should be rewaxed at least annually. Boards can be stored upright against a wall.

Acoustic bells

The acoustic bell is a bell-shaped object made of clear plastic. These environments are designed to increase and encourage vocalization and language. They are very powerful acoustic environments and can be successfully used within English and other National Curriculum areas.

The acoustic bell is placed either above or over the child, with the adult alongside. The adult either waits for the child to make vocalizations, so that he can actively explore the environment independently, or the adult elicits vocalizations by singing simple songs or by saying the child's name.

The acoustic bell can be suspended in the same way as mobiles and can also contain objects within it in the same way as Little Rooms.

The acoustic bell is not readily available from catalogues but can be obtained from the author and Reactive Environments. However, the same properties can be obtained using large buckets and plumbing tanks.

Portable electric fan

This is another interesting and motivating reactive environment. When vocalization is directed into the fan a vibratory echohalic sound is produced, which are loud and unique. For best results, the adult and the child needs to be placed to the side or front of the fan. The effects are surprising and leads to an increase in child's attention, communication and vocalization.

Supporting Children

Environmental platforms

This is the name that I have ascribed to a restricted area with small ridged sides that form a resonance and environmental platform. It creates a personal space around the child, providing security and safety. The approximate size of these platforms depends on the size of the child, but are usually around 98cm in diameter. A plasterer's tray or a cement patch or tuff spot makes an excellent environmental platform. Yellow tape around the outside edge of the tray is useful as an environmental marker.

Therapy balls

These are very enjoyable reactive environments and can elicit much communication. The adult should place the child lying across the ball and start to gently rock the child in a rhythmic manner. A song to accompany this activity is most appropriate. The adult should pause from time to time asking the child to indicate if the activity should be continued or not.

Therapy balls can be purchased from companies like Rompa and Toys for the Handicapped and come in a variety of sizes.

Multi-sensory rooms

These environments are often seen as meaning the same; however, they are very distinctive and produce in many ways different learning outcomes.

They fall into six categories:

- white rooms
- dark rooms
- interactive rooms
- water rooms
- soft-play rooms
- theme rooms.

When considering any of the above rooms, attention needs to be drawn to a number of features.

Planning a multi-sensory room

- *Size.* This is dependent on what you intend to do with the room, how many people will use it and how much space is available in the school. The larger the room, the more equipment is required and the more expensive it will become. Converting a store room into a multi-sensory room is a useful idea, but be careful to consider the following aspects.
- *Colour.* This again depends on its purpose and is very important when considering visual stimulation and enhancement. However, a black or white curtain can combine the effects and benefits of different rooms.

- *Blackout*: This is important, in order to gain the best visual effects. Sunlight can ruin the effects and the session in the room. Correct blackout material is essential for windows (i.e. curtains, roller blinds, black card) and door openings (i.e. use of door seals to prevent light bleed).
- *Furnishings*: This is dependent on the needs of children, but they need to be comfortable and safe. They may need to include soft furnishings for seating (e.g. wedges, rolls and beanbags) and they may need to be wheelchair accessible. However, these environments are good opportunities to take these children out of their wheelchairs and to promote more relaxed body positioning.
- *Equipment*: When designing the room and purchasing equipment it is advisable to talk to a teacher who is experienced in using these rooms and a supplier (e.g. Spacecraft, Rompa) who can give some valuable advice. It is wise not to always buy the cheapest, but to consider the quality, durability and maintenance of the equipment. A decision regarding whether the equipment is to be permanent or mobile also needs to be considered.
- *Safety*: These rooms need to be safe. Padding on lower walls and on the floor is important if children are to be unsupported and independent. There must not be any trailing leads as children and adults will fall over them in the dark. A good supply of power points along each wall and a switch control panel may help. Permanent equipment needs to be harnessed to static furniture or walls.
- *Ventilation*: Good ventilation is important as it makes the rooms more comfortable to be in. Lighting equipment and bodies raise the room temperature and this is especially evident in smaller spaces. Air conditioning and fans are the best option; extractor fans are beneficial but these need to have a low noise feature.
- *Lighting*: It is advisable to have a dimmer switch for room lighting as this will help everyone to adjust from daylight to low light and vice versa.

Room policy

The school needs to write a philosophy or policy for using the room. This will facilitate good practice and avoid misunderstanding. It will need to include:

- named responsible person(s) for advice, cleaning, maintenance and repairs
- ideas on how to use the room
- description of equipment and how to use it
- repairs of equipment (basic safety and maintenance)
- availability and timetable (rota)
- method of recording children's use of the room and setting clear objectives and
- general teaching points (including dos and don'ts).

Always remove footwear or you will have floor tears and equipment damage. It is also advisable not to switch all the equipment on at once, but to use one or two items at a time to avoid visual and sensory bombardment.

White rooms

White rooms are often linked to the philosophy of Snoezelen. This word comes from two Dutch words – 'Snifflen' to smell, 'Doozelen' to sleep or doze. It is a made-up word which has become accepted and used world-wide. Its philosophy is rooted in leisure, pleasure and enjoyment, and focuses on relaxation through gentle stimulation. It is widely used for recuperation and is intended to be non-threatening. Although this philosophy has benefits for children who are multiple disabled, it must not be forgotten that educational outcomes need to be set that do not invariably link to encouraging children to sleep, but to be intellectually and visually stimulated.

The equipment that is commonly found in these rooms is as follows:

- *Lighting* – Solar projector and effects wheels, bubble tubes, fibre-optic sprays and associated products, ultra-violet lights, mirror ball and pinspot, limiglow, light rope nets and flashing lights, reflective and patterned panels
- *Waterbeds*
- *Vibro-tactile equipment* (see next section)
- *Furnishings* – white walls, ceilings and soft play flooring
- *Music* – music system for relaxation music
- *Aromatherapy* – fan or oil-burning lamp or scented candles.

Dark rooms

These rooms are more appropriate for light stimulation sessions. In schools they tend to include converted cupboards, 'Little Rooms', and tables with a thick blanket draped over them. The use of lighting equipment is key to the success of these rooms and its purpose encourages visual enhancement. Children with very little vision are encouraged to use residual vision and develop skills in light awareness, scanning, searching, tracking and fixation.

The equipment that is commonly found in these rooms is as follows:

- *Lighting* – same as the white room. The use of torches with narrow and wide beams accompanied by coloured overlays with a flashing component
- *Furnishings* – black walls and ceilings
- *Television and computers* – these focus on the use of visual stimulation and programmes

Interactive rooms

These have evolved over the past five years from the concepts of both the white and dark rooms. They tend to be very switch-orientated and use equipment solely with a switch basis. The design incorporates a grid of switch sockets around the room under the control of a central switch controller. Sound light floors, infinity tunnels, toys, bubble tubes, tape recorders and sound inset boards may be used. Sessions include periods when the light is on and off. Soft-play equipment is not a major part of these rooms.

6

Water rooms

This is the most expensive type of multi-sensory room and is a more sophisticated version of the white room. It includes an indoor swimming pool and the use of lighting equipment. These rooms incur many safety regulations as well as long-term maintenance fees. Moisture is a big problem causing much erosion to equipment. Large paddling pools can be adapted, although these do have their limitations.

Soft-play rooms

This is a variation of the original soft-play environment equipment. They include ball pools, soft-play furniture, climbing areas and airbeds. They may include light projectors, mirror balls and music. There is a variety of colour schemes; however, they tend to include murals of cartoon characters and light-coloured walls for projector use.

Theme rooms

These are rooms that focus around a theme or a drama. They are similar to white rooms but without the padded flooring. The use of a projector, aromatherapy fans and music systems are key pieces of equipment. A theme will be chosen and will be developed on a multi-sensory design. For example, the theme 'Corfu' may be developed as follows:

- *Sight* – images of waves, sand, blue sky and bathing costumes
- *Sound* – waves, seagulls, Greek music
- *Tactile* – shells, sand, seaweed
- *Smell* – suntan oil, seaweed, garlic and
- *Taste* – salads, taramasalata.

Children and staff may even wear costumes to make the theme more realistic and meaningful.

Vibro-tactile equipment

Children find this reactive environment very rewarding and stimulating. Equipment emits a vibrating pulse that can either be gentle or harsh. The equipment includes massagers, foot spas and vibrating snakes, to name a few examples.

With vibro-cushions and beds, music can be played through them, thus fallowing children to experience music in a tactile way. Children experience a common pulse and what a bass or high note feels like.

A vibro-tactile frame is another piece of equipment that can easily be made. This is a cross in design between the Resonance Board and the Sloping/Tilted Board. The dimensions should measure 85cm high and 60cm long. Hanging from this frame would be similar items used on a

Resonance Board, but they would be attached in a similar way to the Little Room. The function and properties would combine those of a Resonance Board and a Little Room.

Mobiles

The use of mobiles is another effective tool in providing a reactive environment for children with multiple disabilities. They can be made from virtually any objects, as long as they are safe and have no pointed or sharp edges.

They can be lowered to a variety of positions, depending on the needs of the child. They can be placed over the child or at a height to encourage reaching skills. Children can be sitting in chairs or lying down on a Resonance Board to access these environments. When they are not in use they can be raised and fixed securely, providing an effective colourful display. Using a clip-on key-ring allows teachers to interchange mobiles that are no longer required.

Suspended rooms

This environment is a combination of a Little Room, an environmental platform and a mobile. They are easily made from material mounted on a large hoop, that is suspended in the same way as mobiles. They can be placed over a Resonance Board or environmental platform for additional stimulation and for the child to feel additional security.

Switch technology

Switch technology involves any gadgets that allow children, by any movement of their body, to produce an effect which they find pleasing. Switches offer them choices and empower them to control devices that they are unable to hold. Switches can be used for all products which are powered by battery or electricity.

Switches come in a variety of sizes, although it is adviseable to try and find the smallest size switch that the user can access, so as not to interfere with other pieces of equipment.

Switches may be activated by different types of contact, such as up/down, side to side, push or pull, tilting, pressure, squeezing, swiping, suck/blow. Some switches operate on infrared detection, heat, eye movements and breaking a light beam. Some switches are designed for light pressure, while others are for heavy-duty use, such as a foot switch. Some switches offer an adjustment for varying sensitivity. Some require a tiny press while others have to be pressed a long way. Switches should be robust for daily wear and tear.

Switches currently available include the following: leaver; see-saw; jellybean; touch pad; foot; wobble; grasp; thumb; pillow; eye-blink; suck/blow; pressure mat; and joysticks.

There are three types of switch controls. They are:

● *Momentary* – the effects only stay switched on while the child's hand is on the switch.
● *Latched* – this is like a chord-pull bathroom light switch, the effect goes on at the first press and off at the second.
● *Timed* – the effect stays on for a selectable period and then switches off automatically.

Once a switch has been identified, the best method of mounting the switch is required to be established. Some switches may need a complicated bulky mounting system, while others may simply need a piece of velcro. However, always ensure the safety of the child in the use of the equipment. Mount the switch in the best position to meet the optimum physical needs of the child.

Switches can be used for most pieces of equipment. They can include a bubble tube, tape recorder, television, hair dryer, fans, lights, food processor, toys and a Communication Board. Electrical appliances will need to use a device similar to a Powerlink (purchased from Liberator). Battery devices will require a special cable that fits in the battery compartment with a female jack socket to connect the switch (purchased from TFH and Liberator). Other devices on the market that fit within this category are Soundbeam and Midi-Creator.

> **Key points**
> ● Buildings need to be adapted if children who are multiple disabled are to understand and access them independently.
> ● Consider lighting, colour and tone contrast, textural contrast, acoustic conditions, furnishings and general layout.
> ● Reactive environments are important to promote mobility and communication.
> ● Being aware of the whole range of reactive environments and how to use them will enable teachers to provide the child with variable experiences and may provide a key to unlock the door to the child's world.

7 | Mobility and Motor Skills

Joan is nine years old and has encephalitis, cleft lip, cleft palate, light perception and bilateral talipes ('club feet'). She also has epilepsy. Joan enjoys weight-bearing activities and uses a standing frame. She sits and pulls herself up independently and has good head control. She attends a mainstream school with a resourced provision for children who have complex needs. She communicates through a range of sounds and vocalization s. Joan enjoys music and vocalizes melodically. She actively participates and directs the use of a Soundbeam and produces inventive compositions. In school she uses an environmental platform and requires an intervenor to access the curriculum. Her peers love being with her and she loves being with them. When her friends are around Joan, something happens to them and her that words cannot express. Whatever this is, it is something very special.

'The deepest yearning of many children with severe motor difficulties is to run and play with their peers. With appropriate equipment, they can improve their motor skills and achieve some degree of self-directed mobility. This mobility is often the foundation for communication skills, children who cannot pronounce the words to name their desires are able to physically lead others to them.'

Bidabe (1992)

Movement is fundamental to all learning and involves developing motor skills. Our perceptions often influence the way we look at children. We view them differently if they have poor motor skills and are unable to stand, sit or walk independently. Children can be viewed as helpless. These perceptions are transmitted to the children and thus they develop poor self-image and self-esteem. The physical positions they are in also influence their perceptions of themselves and their ability to communicate, move and express themselves. Different positions also provide a different and distorted view of the world in which they live. The world looks very different viewed from the floor or in a wheelchair. Often a child's problem appears to be a motor problem, when in fact it is a motivational one. However, our perceptions and views change if children have some mobile independence.

Movement involves acquiring mobility and orientation skills. Mobility focuses on moving the whole body independently in the environment from one location to another. In Africa, babies experience body motion from birth through being on their mothers' backs. When the mother bends down, they bend down. When she dances, they dance, and so on. Movement is a way to determine and control our life and destiny. Children need to feel empowered, and mobility is an important ingredient to facilitate this. Orientation is the ability to develop a good sense of spatial awareness. This involves knowing where objects are located and the adjustment or alignment of the body in response to them in the environment. Body awareness is an important ingredient of orientation. A child needs to have an understanding of his body parts. He needs to understand that he has two sides to his body, two legs, hands and feet, and that the body starts with the head and ends at his toes. The body can also bend and be manipulated by control of the limbs and this action is not a reflex or something that does not belong to the child.

Many children with multiple disabilities often use some form of echo-location in determining where they are within an environment and what is around them. Echo-location is the ability to locate objects by how sounds are interpreted by the brain. It involves an awareness of sound and how sounds rebound off surfaces, such as walls. It can give information on how far away or how big an object is (e.g. a tree).

Approaches to developing motor skills

Bobath (known as neuro-developmental therapy)
This treatment was developed by Berta and Karel Bobath. They found that through positioning and careful handling, spasticity could be reduced, thus enabling the child to have more control over his own movement. Bobath is an individual-based treatment that may be used if normal development has been interfered with by a brain disorder, or if abnormal patterns of posture and movement are present. It aims to inhibit abnormal postural patterns, therefore facilitating normal muscle tone and movement through repetition and use in everyday life.

Bobath can be carried out anywhere and parents can be taught to use the approach in their day-to-day handling. The disadvantage of this approach is that specialized training is required for the therapist. It is very labour-intensive and much one-to-one support is required. Success also lies in the therapist's skills in handling the child.

Doman-Delacato
This approach was developed by Glen and Robert Doman and Carl Delacato. The main aim of the therapy is to treat the brain by altering the neurological systems within it. It rests on the theory that other parts of the brain will take over functions of the damaged areas if stimulated and uses the technique of patterning and repeating.

The programme uses short sharp bursts of activity that are carried out at regular intervals in exactly the same way, for a number of times a day (three to eight hours in total). Sessions last up to 45 minutes and require at least three supporters.

This approach is probably one of the most controversial therapies available. Prejudice against this approach has arisen from examples such as the suspension of a child upside down in the air held by a rope tied around his feet.

Conductive Education
Andras Peto developed this approach in the 1940s as a system of education which encourages the development of children who are

physically disabled. A 'Conductor' has responsibility for all aspects of the child's education and development. Children are organized into groups, so that they can be motivated to move through peer interaction. Speech and rhythmic intention is used to guide action by speaking out the commands and directing movement and behaviour (e.g. 'I will stand up').

Conductive Education encourages personal development and self-esteem and develops a problem-solving attitude. It aims to make youngsters as independent and as mobile as possible.

MOVE (Mobility Opportunities Via Education)

MOVE is a philosophy and is not a therapy or treatment. It is a way of thinking about and teaching mobility and movement in a functional and life-situation context. It was first developed in the early 1980s by Linda Bidabe, a special education teacher in Bakersfield, California, USA. In 1990, she published a curriculum guide and profile in order that it could be more widely used. International MOVE trainers provide training to institutions and parents, so that the philosophy and programme can be effectively implemented.

MOVE aims to increase independence, freedom and mobility, and in so doing enhances the dignity and good health of people with disabilities through innovative thinking, training and collaborative teamwork. It asserts that movement is the basic foundation for learning.

MOVE encourages functional movement through use of everyday life skills and tasks, and appropriate equipment. It increases the self-esteem of the disabled child by increasing independence and enabling him to view the world from the same physical plane and perspective as his peers. It moves away from passive motor activities (i.e. lying and sitting) to interactive movement.

MOVE provides a structure for teaching and integrating motor skills into the curriculum in an inclusive way, focusing on sitting, standing and walking. It also provides an effective way of recording functional motor skills, as well as physical prompts, and can easily be incorporated into a child's individual educational programme and the National Curriculum. This approach is growing in its popularity and use in schools across the UK and Europe, as well as the USA.

Motor development

Babies quickly learn to counteract the effects of gravity and to balance. Although developmentalists talk about stages or milestones, motor skills tend to happen simultaneously and stages are not always completed before moving onto the next. Some babies even miss out stages altogether (e.g. some don't learn to crawl, they move from sitting to standing and then to walking).

However, an understanding of motor development does equip us with an invaluable assessment tool to enable identification of delay or abnormal movement patterns. Stages or milestones of motor development which are usually achieved in the first 12–18 months of life incorporate the following:

● prone (lying on the front)
● supine (lying on the back)
● crawling
● sitting
● standing
● walking.

Reflexes

Babies are born with many different reflexes; some are more significant than others. Normal reflexes include sucking, rooting, placing, reflex walking, the moro and startle reflexes and the palmar and plantar grasps. The moro and rooting reflexes are present in the newborn. Other reflexes indicate abnormality by their weakness, absence, excessive strength, or persistence to an abnormal age. The palmar grasp reflex is normal until about three months, but persistence indicates a problem and interferes with the development of the hand function.

Asymmetrical Tonic Neck Reflexes (ATNR) are present in newborn babies but can have major effects if they persist and are not counteracted. This is common in children with physical disabilities.

Righting and balance reactions

The emergence of righting and balance reactions is very important the acquisition of motor development and usually occurs in the first 18 months of life. These reactions are rooted in the vestibular and proprioceptive sense (see Chapter 4). The righting reaction is automatic but is an active response to maintaining the normal upright position of the body in space. It keeps the head upright, the face vertical and mouth horizontal. The balance reaction is also a highly automatic response to changes in posture and movement, aimed at restoring balance. It consists of saving, stepping and tilting reactions.

Physiotherapy

The role of physiotherapists is to encourage and develop motor skills and to inhibit any abnormal motor responses. Within this role, they will use their skills of assessment and knowledge of any underlying medical condition to devise a programme of therapeutic activities, to maintain and develop a child's motor skills.

The programme a physiotherapist could implement may follow developmental guidelines that rely on the child mastering one skill before moving on to the next, but also should consider the functional skills required for independence. The programme generally focuses on increasing muscle strength and control, sequencing movement patterns and controlling and preventing dysfunction, weakness and deformity. It provides exercises to help with easing restraint and fatigue through use of equipment (e.g. wheelchairs, standing frames and fully supported seating). Inhibiting abnormal movement is paramount and is seen as a preventative or delaying treatment. It is important that any physiotherapy programme incorporates functional daily living skills, if it is to be fully meaningful to the child.

Many children with multiple disabilities fail to progress to independent functional skills (such as sitting, standing and walking) if a developmental model is solely applied because of the stage the child is at in their development or because of deformity. If a child becomes badly deformed, many difficulties arise (e.g. they may be unable to sit or move and their body may become twisted). Exercises are used to encourage normal movement and prevent deformity. Another cause of deformity is gravity and poor vestibular control. Deformity can be seen as a result of wrong messages coming from the brain to muscles and joints – this is particularly true of children with cerebral palsy.

A treatment cycle that a physiotherapist might use can be seen below:

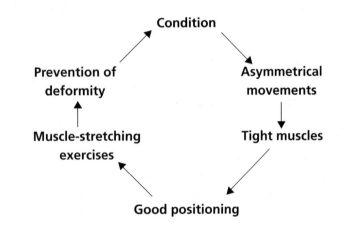

Many children hold asymmetrical positions and postures. This is when the positioning of one side of the body is different from that on the other side. Asymmetrical movements lead to stiffness, uncomfortable positioning and deformity. Often children are tightly harnessed into their equipment to reduce the risk of deformity. However, this sends messages to the child that he should not move but remain still. It also encourages children to rely on the harnesses or prompts to carry out basic body movement, such as head and trunk control.

Stretching

Stretching can be provided as a therapeutic corrective exercise and to prepare children prior to placing them in equipment. There is a lot of controversy about how effective stretches are in lengthening or even maintaining muscle length. Many argue that standing and walking are the most natural and productive forms of stretching muscles. However, what is of paramount importance is that tight muscles are eased and 'warmed up' before placing children into equipment.

The range of stretching exercises tends to fall into three muscle categories: psoas muscle, tendon achilles and hamstrings. The psoas muscle is found at the front of the thigh. The tendon achilles is the tendon cord found at the back of the heel and this is a common trouble spot for children. Hamstrings are very long muscles found on the back of the thigh. They cross two joints; the hip and knee and are often at risk of getting tight.

It is not advisable to stretch children without the advice of the physiotherapist. Children have varying medical problems and teachers and support workers should be shown how to stretch individual children. Inappropriate handling can cause injury and damage, as well as giving the child much stress, discomfort and pain.

Equipment

Following an assessment it may be decided that a range of equipment is required to facilitate motor skills. When considering the use of equipment it is very important to seek the advice of the physiotherapist in order to correctly position the child, as inappropriate positioning can lead to damage, discomfort and pain. There are numerous manufacturers of equipment and they include Camp, Coopers, Leckey, Rifton, Tyco and Quest 88.

Types of equipment will be considered under four categories: sitting, standing, walking and other.

Sitting

Good seating and positioning is important for all children, especially those with multiple difficulties. A good seating position is to have approximately 90 degree angles at the ankles, knees and hips, with the back of the chair in a slightly forward-leaning position. The specialist chairs range from those that have an adjustable height,to ones that tilt, ergonomical classroom chairs, corner floor sitters and wheelchairs. Many come with a variety of straps, head and footrests, knee blocks and pommels.

Chairs
Chairs should be designed for good independent seating and provide the correct angled support to the child's body. A child can sit in these independently, have a strap around the hips, or be physically supported from behind by an adult.

Chairs with an adjustable height and tilting chairs can provide total to partial support while the child is in a seating position. This is achieved through a variety of strappings, pommels, adjustable sides and backs, head and foot rests, and can be reduced as the child becomes more independent in supporting his own body. They provide good seating and positioning and are useful for all school activities including lunchtime. However, sometimes they are quite large and often are unable to fit under standard school tables. An adjustable table may be the solution in this case.

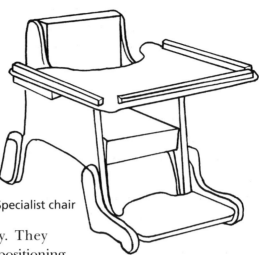

Specialist chair

There are a range of Corner Floor Sitters. These come in a variety of shapes and sizes, with and without pommels and straps. They are particularly useful when children are unable to sit on the floor independently (e.g. for Circle Time and the Literacy Hour). The child can sit with his peers, rather than above them or set back from the main group.

Wheelchairs

These come in a range of designs depending on the physical support needs of the child. Some may incorporate spinal moulds shaped in the design of the child's spine and back to avoid deformity, with a range of strappings, knee blocks and head and foot rests. Others may only have a hip harness.

It is very important not to move children in wheelchairs without telling them why they are being moved. Children require time to prepare themselves for the move and for their route to be interpreted while they are being taken. Verbal interpretation is very important. However, if they have hearing difficulties then using a body sign (e.g. a touch on the shoulder) similar to an object of reference, may indicate that they are going to move. They will soon acquire meaning to this sign if it is consistently applied.

Supporting sitting

When placing the child in a supported sitting position and placing him back into a wheelchair, it is important to remember appropriate manual-handling procedures. Although it can be a very positive experience for the child to sit on the floor next to his peers, it can place the adult's own health at risk. Strains and back problems can develop as a result of inappropriate handling. It is always advisable when placing children in these positions to seek the advice of a professional who specializes in manual-handling training.

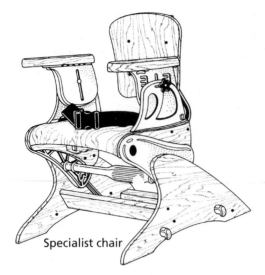

Specialist chair

How the child is supported on the floor is dependent upon his physical condition as well as his individual skills and abilities. Some may require full support, while their others need partial support in the form of providing help with their balance.

If the child requires full support, the adult will need to be behind him, with the child's legs in between the adult's. Place the child's bottom as close to the adult as possible and support his trunk by holding him. If possible, cross the legs of the child and enfold them within the adult's crossed legs. Try to encourage the child to be forward leaning, as this will help him to gain greater control of his head and trunk, and his arms and hands will be more relaxed and controlled. If the child requires partial support, the adult may need to sit to the side, with his arm around the child's trunk or shoulders or holding his legs.

Standing

The benefits of placing a child in a standing position include the following:

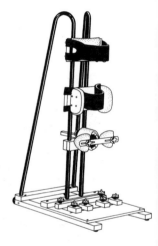

Standing frame

- It is a good position to maximize the benefits stretching trunk and leg muscles.
- It is a weight-bearing position, which promotes growth and strength.
- It promotes development of the hip joint.
- It provides a position of symmetry.
- It helps to improve head control.

Equipment that promotes standing includes the standing frame prone standing frame, supine board, and dynamic stander.

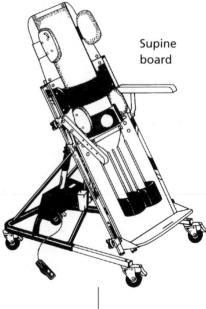

Supine board

The standing frame

A standing frame is a static piece of equipment which supports a child in a standing position. It consists of the following: a base support for feet; two side poles; knee block; pelvic strap; thoracic strap; and tray.

7

Prone stander

Dynamic stander

Supine board and prone standing frame

These pieces of equipment are particularly useful for those who are unable to weight-bear sufficiently. They are used for children with poor or variable head control or with scoliosis. In addition, they are beneficial for those children who have too much extension or who cannot tolerate full weight-bearing through their legs. The supine board is sometimes referred to as a tilt table.

The dynamic stander

The advantage of a dynamic stander is that it allows the child to be in a mobile, upright position instead of a fixed and stationary one. It can also be used as a static standing frame. This piece of equipment enables children to play with other children in the playground and similar environments while in a normal upright position. It enhances social integration and improves peer perceptions of the child, as well as increasing self-esteem.

Walking

There are a number of benefits to encouraging children to walk:

- It promotes a weight-bearing position and standing balance.
- It improves head control, arm function and reciprocal leg movements.
- It promotes all the benefits of a standing position.
- It promotes physical exercise and health.
- It provides an opportunity to walk and run similar to that of their peers.
- It strengthens and stretches muscles.
- It raises self-esteem.
- It increases blood flow of the whole body, as well as respiration.
- It helps avoid constipation problems.
- It is the way that most people get from one place to another place.

The range of equipment that is available to promote walking includes hand support frames and rollators, postural control walkers, gait trainers, lift walkers and walking prompts.

Hand support frames and rollators

Hand support frames are frames made from aluminium which generally have no straps or wheels. In order to move forward, the child is required to lift the lightweight frame forward to walk and then to repeat this process to get to a pre-determined destination. Rollators are similar to hand support frames, but are different in that there are wheels on the frame. The frame is in front of the child and the handles are height-adjustable. The frames are made from aluminium and have no straps or supports on them. Rollators require the child to use the strength in his arms to reduce the amount of weight taken through his legs in a balanced support. Some rollators look like a tricycle, with three wheels and brakes. Rollators can be quite difficult to manipulate and control, although they are easier to use than hand support frames.

Postural control walkers

These walkers place the handgrips on either side of the child, with the cross rails behind the child. They are designed to eliminate many of the problems of alignment, while facilitating a more positive gait. The walkers usually combine a folding aluminium frame with height adjustable legs. The legs can be fitted with wheels. They allow easier access to tables and work surfaces.

Gait trainers

Gait trainers are similar to rollators and consist of a metal frame on wheels, which the child stands in, surrounded by a number of adjustable straps and prompts to support the trunk, legs, arms and hip.

Walking prompts

There are a variety of aids to support walking such as walking sticks and crutches. There are a number of different walking sticks to choose from. They include the traditional wooden canes or aluminium adjustable rod, the tripod (three prongs) and quadrapod (four prongs) rods. They provide a valuable prompt and are useful for those children who can take weight through their arm but require some physical and balance support and stability.

Other equipment

The wedge

The wedge provides a supportive base in a prone or front lying position. There are a number of benefits in using a wedge and they include the following:

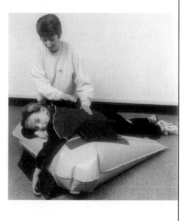

- It promotes active use of back and neck muscles.
- It provides a possibility of weight-bearing through the arms.
- It is a position of symmetry.
- It encourages better head control.
- It allows muscles to be stretched.

A wedge is a triangular block made of soft, cushioned material. Children are placed on it without any further support or by using a variety of supports that include a pelvic strap, a chest strap or abduction block.

Side-lying boards

The reasons for using this equipment include the following:

- It stops the child from pushing back.
- It keeps the shoulders forward and allows the hands to keep to the body mid-line.
- If a child has asymmetrical tonic neck reflex it can help the child to be more symmetrical.

This is a piece of equipment that places a child in a correct side-lying position. It involves a long soft-padded board with strappings and small wedges with velcro. It may be necessary to use pillows to ensure that the legs are adequately supported. It is also important to be aware of the child's line of vision if active involvement and inclusion is to be encouraged.

Tricycles

These are useful for therapy and mobility around the school and the community. However, because of their size, their use is restricted indoors as they are too large. They provide the child with an opportunity to experience motion, speed and direction, as well as independent movement.

Orthotics

These are mechanical aids that assist and enable the person to produce movement safely and correctly. This equipment mainly includes strappings and splints: a splint is a layman's term for a variety of equipment that includes angle-foot orthoses (AFOs), hand and finger splints and gaiters. The purpose of splints is to support, stretch and fix joints in to position. AFOs tend to be lightweight and are usually made of polythene plastic with foam-padded edges with adjustable fasteners. Gaiters are made of cloth material with metal bars inside them and are mainly used on legs and arms.

Therapy rolls and balls

Both these pieces of equipment can be purchased from companies like Camp, Quest 88, Coopers, Rompa and Toys for the Handicapped and come in a variety of sizes. The equipment is commonly used to improve a child's posture and balance and to encourage and shape symmetrical body positions.

Hoists

The main types of hoists available include the mobile hoist with either a strap or boom system, the mobile-foldable and transportable hoist, and the track hoist. Mobile hoists with a strap are useful for transfers from wheelchairs to the toilet, floor, bed, or from sitting to standing,

7

and can be used for walking. The boom hoists are useful for low lifting, seat-to-seat, toilet and changing plinth transfers. Some can lift on and off the floor. Most foldable versions are lightweight and are easily stored and transported by car. A track hoist system can either be fixed to the ceiling, walls or be freestanding on wheels. They can be single track with a fixed route or H (sometimes known as XY) track, which covers the whole room. The fixed track system is very useful in limited space. The freestanding system is useful for more single purposes (i.e. access to a ball pool) or if there is a need to change its location.

Manual handling

Currently there is much concern and controversy over how adults are handling and lifting children. There is a shift of attention away from the child and the focus is instead placed on the risk to the adult in the situation, rather than the future independence of the child. There are fears that this could lead to more dependency on lifting equipment and more children either remaining in wheelchairs or not being placed in equipment. However, it is important that the school follows a manual handling policy initiated by the council or school for the safety and protection of the pupils and staff.

Currently there is much concern and controversy over how adults are handling and lifting children. There is a shift of attention away from the child and the focus is instead placed on the risk to the adult

The Manual Handling Operations Regulations 1992 incorporates the Health and Safety at Work Act 1974 and the European Commission Guidelines on safe manual-handling practice. The regulations define handling as:

'The supporting or transporting of a load by hand or bodily force. This includes pushing and carrying to support, lift or lower any load.' The regulations state a clear hierarchy of measures within the three aspects: Avoid, Assess, Reduce (AAR). Support staff should avoid hazardous manual-handling tasks whenever possible by altering the task to avoid moving the child or by using mechanical means. They should assess any hazardous task that cannot be avoided and they should reduce the risk of injury as far as is reasonably practicable.

Jackson (1998) outlined a number of factors and guidelines to follow in risk assessment, including the task, the individual and the environment.

The task

Consider the following points:

● Does it need to be done?
● Does it involve twisting, stooping and bending?
● Is it repetitive?
● Does it involve more than one person?

- Does it mean carrying a child for long distances?
- Does it involve lowering the child accurately?
- Does it involve holding the child away from the trunk?
- Does it involve sudden movement?

The individual

Consider the handler's:

- health
- age and sex
- physical abilities and inabilities
- strength
- height and weight
- existing injuries
- knowledge, skills, training and experience.

The environment

Consider the following:

- the ease of access
- the route
- flooring type and variations in level
- obstacles and barriers
- heat, humidity or cold
- time of the day
- height restrictions
- other people within the area.

Jackson (1998) also outlined some main principles of safe handling:

- Always use appropriate equipment if it is available.
- Assess the child and find out about the method to move them.
- Explain what you are doing.
- Prepare the handling area and watch for all hazards.
- Know your lifting capacity.
- Always lift towards yourself, never away from you.
- Always hold the child as close as possible to you.
- Use your own body weight to balance and move the child.
- Do not twist your own trunk when lifting.
- Relax your knees and raise your head as you lift to maintain an erect spine.
- Use rhythm and timing when lifting and do not jerk.
- Always use clear instructions (e.g. Ready – Steady – Go).

The following lifts are now considered illegal and should not be used:

- *The drag lift*: two people either side of the child, using the crook of the elbows to lift the child under his armpit and the child is then dragged backwards to the desired position.

- *The cradle lift*: two people either side of the child, linking through the child from behind. The child is lifted on clasped wrists and the handlers have to lean forward to prevent falling.
- *The hammock transfer*: one handler passes their arms under the child's shoulders from behind, folding the child's arms across his chest. The second handler holds the child's legs.

Handling equipment

There is a wide range of equipment and each item should always be viewed in terms of its intended purpose. The equipment available includes the following:

- *Side and glide sheet*: thin nylon material, which allows sliding in two directions.
- *One-way slide sheet*: anti-slip mat designed to move in one direction only.
- *Transfer board*: tapered at either end and used to slide a child from one level to another.
- *Turning discs*: made of two circular discs that rotate against one another and acts as a turntable.
- *Handling swings*: made of flexible plastic with built-in handles.
- *Handling belts*: made from adjustable webbing with vertical and horizontal handholds.
- *Hand blocks*: blocks with handles made from material or plastic.
- *Hoists*: a lifting device that can be operated manually or electronically.

The importance of working together in regard to correct handling can facilitate more normal movement and inhibit the use and reinforcement of abnormal development patterns. It provides a consistent forward approach and the child makes significant progress as a result.

Risk Assessment

For many, risk assessment creates anxiety and concern. However, this does not need to be so. Simply, risk assessment is a careful examination of the environment or situation that could cause harm to the child and those supporting him, in order to weigh up whether enough precautions are necessary. The aim is to make sure that no one gets hurt, and that hazards are reduced by satisfactory precautions so that the risk is small. Risk assessment is not about saying no to an action but it is about saying how we can make the action safer for the child and his support worker.

A risk assessment should be recorded in a formal document consisting of the following:

- A description of the situation and those involved.
- A list of the hazards.
- A list of potential risks.
- A list of existing precautions and additional precautions required to reduce the risks.

The cradle lift

The hammock transfer

7

- A record of precautions implemented (including training).
- A review date.
- A signature of the assessor and school representative.

For further information contact the Health & Safety Executive.

Key points
- Movement is fundamental to all learning. All children yearn to sit, stand, walk and run. A parent's desire is for her child to do these things.
- Motor skills need to be practised as part of everyday life and not taught in isolation or at particular times on the timetable. Movement is a way of life and developing motor skills needs to follow within natural and functional situations.
- For many children who are multiple disabled, following a traditional method based on normal developmental milestones often means that they may never stand or walk. However, using other approaches and methods challenges our way of thinking about teaching motor skills and may open the door to facilitate independent mobility.
- There is a wide range of equipment available to help children with mobility. A team approach which includes the parents is very important in the selection of any equipment. Advice from a physiotherapist or occupational therapist should always be sought before using any equipment.
- No exercises should be followed without the advice of a physiotherapist, as misuse can lead to body damage and pain.
- A team approach involving the parents is essential in planning and developing the acquisition of motor skills.
- Knowing the correct manual-handling techniques is essential, in order to ensure the safety of the children and adults. Appropriate advice should always be sought from a professional who specializes in manual handling.

7

8 Support frameworks in mainstream education

Gill is 15 years old and attends a mainstream school. When she was 13 she was diagnosed as having Niemann-Pick Disease. She is ambulant and intellectually communicates her needs, views and intentions. She uses a crowding frame reducer, bold-lined paper, pens, large print and a blue overlay. This minimizes her visual perceptual difficulties. Gill loves animals and makes her preferences known regarding fashion and music. Although her physical skills are deteriorating, her motivation is high and she enjoys the social interaction of her peers and adults. Gill fully participates in lessons alongside her peers and will sit her GCSEs and national examinations at the appropriate time.

Facilitating inclusive education

'Inclusion is a process which recognizes that impairment and disability are common to all and values the individual as a person, enabling access, equality and achievement. It is about a whole school policy where the community accepts and values diversity.'

Pickles (1999)

Inclusion is a term that has been and is used in a positive and negative ways. However, the essence of inclusion is that communities accept, support, tolerate and appreciate one another, and that no grouping is rejected or segregated. This should be true regardless of their culture, ethniticity, gender, sexuality and ability. Few would disagree that a person's right to equal opportunity and inclusive societies is a basic human right. The right for all children to learn together and that children should not be devalued or discriminated against by being excluded, sent away or placed into separate establishments because of their disability are key issues for an inclusive society. Children do not need to be protected from each other and there is no legitimate reason to separate children for their education. Children belong together, with advantages and benefits for all. Segregation teaches children and society to be fearful and ignorant and breeds prejudice. Inclusive education has the potential to reduce barriers and fears and promotes friendships, respect, acceptance, understanding and cooperation. All children need a mainstream education that will help them to develop relationships and prepare them for life.

Inclusive environments give opportunity for children with multiple disabilities and peers to learn about and from each other. The Centre for Studies on Inclusive Education (CSIE) shows all disabled children do better academically and socially in education. Teaching standards are found to be higher and learning approaches are more diverse and this benefits all children. Good inclusive practice in schools is essential if success is to be facilitated.

'Inclusive Education describes the process by which a school attempts to respond to all pupils as individuals by reconsidering and restructuring its curricular organisation and provision and allocating resources to enhance equality of opportunity. Through this process, the school builds its ccapacity to accept all pupils from the local community who wish to attend and, in doing so, reduces the need to exclude pupils.'

Sebba and Sachder (1997)

The term 'inclusive education' includes:

- The placement of pupils with special educational needs in mainstream schools.
- The participation of all pupils in the curriculum and social life of mainstream schools.
- The participation of all pupils in learning which leads to the highest possible level of achievement.
- The participation of young people in a full range of social experiences and opportunities once they have left school.

Inclusive education makes it necessary to review how people are treated. It encompasses equal opportunities and equal rights issues, as well as making society confront the notions of what is meant by 'ordinary' and 'normal'. Inclusion attempts to meet the needs of every pupil, valuing and respecting diversity and difference.

Inclusive education is rooted in the belief that inclusion is an entitlement for all children and that it is a logical extension of the principles of comprehensive education. It promotes the idea that good practice is concerned with the delivery of differentiated teaching and learning and this helps to raise educational achievements for *all* pupils.

Inclusive education reduces fear and promotes friendship, respect, understanding and cooperation. Inclusion is about belonging to a community where all children can learn. It encompasses different races, religions, aspirations and disabilities. It increases self-esteem, understanding, tolerance and respect.

In most countries around the world, a committment in legislation to inclusion is clearly evident. In England, legislation such as the Children's Act (1989), Education Act (1993, 2005), Green Paper (1997, 2002), Special Educational Needs and Disability Act (SENDA 2000) and Disability and Discrimination Act (DDA 1995, 2005) all promote inclusion and equal opportunity for all people in society. The current legislation (2006) promotes a strategy that 'Every Child

Matters' and upholds the basic right and entitlement to a broad, balanced and differentiated curriculum for all pupils.

There is an increasing expectation that the majority of pupils with special needs will attend their neighbourhood school and that schools will develop their own expertise, with the support of the peripatetic services. However, there are arguments for centres of excellence in resourced schools, serving groups of children requiring a particular type of support. For some local authorities, this is considered to be the best way of achieving inclusion. For others, this is a necessary compromise on the way to inclusion.

Inclusion builds on the good practice that already exists. It is important to develop whole-school approaches to inclusion as both a social model and a means of raising standards and achievements.

Traditional classroom activities are unlikely to motivate children with multiple disabilities or provide them with appropriate opportunities to develop language and a sense of control. The pace of activities and rate of progression from one topic to another can lead to confusion and insecurity. Communication can be too abstract and complex. Environments can be inflexible and not individually designed. Therefore, staff will need specific training and experience, and a repertoire of appropriate skills. Staff need to know that they will be given the information they need at the different stages of a pupil's development. Pupils require a school committed to individualized programmes.

The ultimate goal of inclusive education is to make it possible for every child, whatever their special needs may be, to attend their neighbourhood or mainstream school. Children need to have the opportunity to gain full access to a broad and balanced curriculum within the National Curriculum, to participate in every aspect of mainstream life and to achieve their potential.

Sebba and Sachdev (1997) stated that inclusion involves a change in teacher, pupil and parent attitudes from a focus on the disability to the appreciation of the person. For teachers, the process of inclusion is a more powerful basis for teacher development and good practice than most in-service training.

Inclusion requires teaching strategies that enable all pupils to participate and learn from one another and to be with each other for as much time as possible. It involves a variety of teacher techniques and strategies that are of benefit to all pupils. It is much more than just differentiating materials.

There must be time for and commitment to quality joint planning between teachers and support staff. Classroom support needs to be used flexibly to ensure it enhances rather than impedes the process.

8

The first step of inclusive education is shared ownership of the process: for teachers to recognize and accept that all the pupils in their class are individuals, and that the focus is on finding ways for all children to access the curriculum.

Listening to each other and respecting different views, including those of non-teaching staff, are the keys to working together. Positive attitudes of staff, children and their parents to inclusive education are crucial in developing provision for multiple-disabled pupils.

Pupil participation and learning can be enriched and enhanced by maximizing peer support, referring to the pupil's concrete experiences and having high realistic expectations. Peer tutoring, cooperative group work, 'buddying', pupils providing feedback to teachers about teaching effectiveness, and initiatives such as Circle of Friends are important tools in facilitating inclusion.

Peer acceptance is important. It is invariably linked to social interaction and this is more easily achieved in the pupils' early years. The process of inclusion therefore needs to be started at an early age so that pupils grow up with it and see it as a normal process of education.

Some parents of children with multiple disabilities may think that their children will not make the same gains in inclusive education as pupils in mainstream education. Research shows the opposite is true. Pupils make academic gains, as well as social, interpersonal and personal gains. Inclusive education enriches the environment for all children.

Education, health authorities and adult services need to develop ways of working together and to be prepared to change, learn and take on new challenges if inclusive education is to succeed. This process will take time, commitment and the allocation of appropriate funds, particularly to support children in their early years.

If schools are willing to provide inclusion for these children, then a radical shift of emphasis in management and policy must ideally take place. Learning needs to be carefully planned and structured. Environments need specific requirements and layout. Resources, both human and material, need to be available to provide advice and support to staff and pupils. Local authorities and schools will need to fully embrace a philosophy of inclusive education and equal opportunity and to commit funding that delivers high-quality learning outcomes for all pupils, irrespective of their abilities (even if it affects 'SATs' results). Funding will need to be protected or 'ring-fenced' for these pupils. Effective teamwork and a close working relationship with multi-disciplinary agencies and support services is integral to the success of inclusion. Schools will need to work closer with parents and establish effective partnership strategies and support mechanisms.

8

It is clear from legislation that local authorities should strive to promote and implement a policy of inclusive education; however, with the focus on obtaining higher national examination results, within a tightly controlled funding mechanism, these will be difficult to fully support and implement.

Support frameworks

The way the school is organized to support children, and how this support is implemented, underpins whether the child will succeed or fail. These organizational frameworks will need to be clear and consistent. They will need to promote an ethos of communication, particularly where there is a staff changeover, and be informative, demonstrating pupil progression and difficulties. This can then be coordinated by the class teacher and the school's special educational needs coordinator.

A support framework model to facilitate inclusion could be the one shown below. This process model will be unpacked through the rest of the chapter.

Support Framework Model

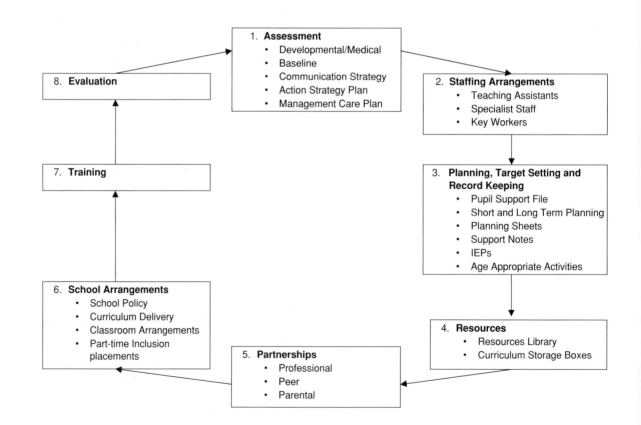

1 Assessment

This first stage is very important, as it will inform us of our direction. It will include a general assessment (developmental and medical), a Baseline Assessment, a Communication Strategy, an Action Strategy Plan and a Management Care Plan. Some of these topics have already been discussed in Chapter 5.

Action strategy plan

This will consist of basic information on how the child can access lessons. It should be summarized onto one side of A4 and should include the following:

- environmental considerations (i.e. lighting, classroom arrangement)
- seating position in relation to the teacher and blackboard, for group work, carpet time and assembly
- position of peers and support staff for group work
- distance for reading the blackboard and viewing demonstrations
- reading and print size
- adaptation of materials, resources and worksheets
- mode of communication
- support equipment.
- P.E. requirements
- ICT access.

Management care plans (MCP)

This is a very important and essential document that outlines the management arrangements in supporting a child with their personal care needs. It becomes a legal document, written by professionals with the full knowledge and support of the school nurse and parents. When complete, it should be signed by a school representative, school nurse and parent. Its lifespan should be one year, with a review date after six months. It should be re-written each year with additional new information. It is an invalid document if it has not been signed by a parent or medical person (as this signifies their understanding of the method of support being implemented). If there is no MCP and an accident occurs, this could lead to a claim of negligence.

The MCP should include the following sections:

- *general information* – date of birth, home address, parents names, school, family and emergency phone numbers, school nurse
- *medical information* – vision, hearing, medication, diabetic, allergies
- *staff support* – teacher, intervenor, teaching assistant, SENCO, lunchtime worker, transport driver and escort
- *special condition* – description, daily requirements, emergency plan, staff responsible
- *mobility* – equipment used and handling arrangements
- *meal times* – utensils used, how they are to be implemented, staff responsible

- *toilet arrangements* – handling, use of gloves, changing pads, use of hoist
- *physiotherapy programme* – attached to the document
- *general safety* – any other aspects not included:
  Signatures, date and review date.

2 Staffing arrangements

Teaching Assistants (TAs)

The role of the TA is crucial for the successful integration of multiple disabled children. It is a complex role, which involves many skills. These include:

- the use of intervenor skills
- differentiation of materials
- direct support to access lessons
- liaising with staff
- helping in setting targets
- implementing IEPs
- possibly also carrying out physiotherapy exercises.

According to Fox (1993) the role of the TA with pupils is to promote independence, inspire confidence and trust, foster peer-group acceptance and enable and empower the child. Their role in relation to teachers is to work in partnership with them, to provide feedback about the pupil, to help in setting targets, to monitor and evaluate programmes and record information. Their role within the school is to work as part of a team, to contribute to child reviews, to know and follow school procedures and to attend relevant in-service training or staff meetings.

In addition to the above skills, they are expected to be patient, flexible, caring, sensitive and enthusiastic. In many ways, they are expected to be 'super people'. However, despite these expectations, TAs are still fulfilling their duties with little training, poor pay and without a proper career structure. If TAs are to develop and evolve their own unique identity as supporters of children, it will be necessary for their job to be professionally recognized and valued.

Key workers

These are usually non-teaching support workers who are the named person for providing regular support to specific children. They would either be an Intervenor, Nursery Nurse or TA. Their role would be similar to the role of an TA and, in addition, they would be responsible for ensuring the making of appropriate materials and communicating with other staff for that specific child.

Specialist staff

It is important that specialist staff with the necessary skills and expertise are employed to assess, provide direct support and give advice

8

regarding the needs of the pupil. These professionals should also be skilled in developing good inclusive practice. These professionals could include specialist teachers for pupils with special educational needs, or teachers of the deaf or visually impaired or with specific learning difficulties, as well as physiotherapists, speech therapists and occupational therapists.

3 Planning, Target-Setting and Record-Keeping

Pupil support file

A good method of coordinating and collating work is through a pupil support file system. This file could be in an A4 binder and include the following sections:

- general information (i.e. the names of the key worker and support teachers, and other professionals involved)
- medical and professional information (i.e. medical details/report, advice of the physiotherapist, speech therapist, occupational therapist)
- their statement of educational need
- specific programmes (i.e. physiotherapy, speech therapy, toileting and feeding programmes)
- an action strategy plan outlining specific ways a child can access the curriculum and environment
- a timetable showing times when the child will receive support.
- a weekly planning and record sheet
- weekly support notes
- an Individual Educational Programme (IEP) and evaluation notes
- short-term planning record sheet
- long-term planning notes.

Using this system, the class teacher will always be able to track the child's acheivements and be aware of progress or difficulties being encountered. It will also facilitate organization problems and identify areas needing attention and further support or times when support can be reduced. These aspects must always be within the mindset of those working with the child.

Short- and long-term planning

All teachers in mainstream education plan meticulously for the class, however, the planning for the child with multiple disabilities may not be of the same detail and can often be tagged onto the end of the planning session. Engaging TAs and the class teacher in planning and day-to-day work of pupils is key to the future success of the inclusion of these pupils and to increase their achievement and progression. However, if planning for these children is to be truly effective, then quality time needs to be allocated on a weekly basis to teachers, TAs and key workers. It will also need to include short-/ medium- and long-term planning. Short-term planning would include either weekly planning and record sheets (see p. 159), daily support notes, a short-term subject planning sheet (see p. 160), the making of resources, establishing aims, objectives and activities to deliver the curriculum and incorporating long-term planning. Long-term planning involves writing IEPs, seeking advice from professionals, developing resources, planning visits, making risk assessments, funding, training, and establishing peer group partnerships and support network groups.

When planning work, always start with the learning needs of the pupils, build activities into the teacher's termly plan, plan activities as a timetabled part of the curriculum and consider inclusion at every activity (including pupil/peer involvement). Teachers should always give support staff plenty of time to differentiate materials, as this task is very time consuming.

Record-keeping

Meaningful record-keeping will need to be continuous rather than occasional. Ticks boxes are insufficient as the recording process needs to be broader. Make a record after each session, as thoughts will be fresh and facts will not be forgotten. Regular record-keeping meetings to discuss progress are also important. Keep record-keeping systems simple and quick to complete. Also consider other methods of recording progress such as photo of work and video recordings.

Weekly planning sheet

This is a written timetable of all the activities the child will do each day. It will identify the subject and tasks for each portion of the day and will provide space alongside each portion for comments. Depending on its complexity, it can either be formatted on A4 or A3 paper. A sample of weekly planning sheets can be seen on page 159. These sheets will help to facilitate communication between staff and will provide a working structure for National Curriculum tasks and IEP targets. They will need to be constructed the week before so that resources are in place for the Monday morning. Used carefully, they will inform teachers of the child's achievements throughout the day and facilitate liaising when support is transferred to other staff. Parents can also be given a copy of this to reinforce language and other work followed in school. The short-term planning sheet (p. 160) enables staff to plan a block of sessions regarding a subject, and evaluate progression and future progress.

Support notes

Support notes are required in order to provide information to the class teacher and support staff about the performance of the child, highlighting strengths and weaknesses. They can also be used to indicate a child's behaviour and arousal level. If these are completed correctly at the end of the lesson, they should take no longer than one minute. When support staff come to support a child they should look at this first to update themselves about how the well the child has got on so far that day. They will also give information to the intervenor to discuss with the child.

Support notes will provide another valuable way to track progress, which can be used at the end of the week for IEP evaluation. They will

8

Weekly planning sheet

_____   _____
(Month)   (Name)

Mon					
Tues					
Wed					
Thurs					
Fri					

Weekly record support sheet

_____   _____
(Month)   (Name)

Mon					
Tues					
Wed					
Thurs					
Fri					

Short-term planning sheet

Subject

Name of pupil

Date	Key objectives	Activities & experiences	Evaluation & outcomes

Individual education plan

Name of pupil _____ Class _____ Start date _____ Review date _____

No.	Objectives (and methods)		Date: Comments	Date: Comments	Date: Comments	Date: Comments

aslo give support staff accountability, as well as providing a record of support from day to day and week to week. An example of a weekly record support sheet can be found on page 159. An A3 format is advisable and these can be folded within the file.

Individual Educational Programmes (IEPs)

An IEP is a scheme of work that consists of small graded steps which relate to the child's individual needs and builds on what they can already do. Its purpose is to enable the child to make progress. It needs to be relevant, explicit, not complicated, and possible to evaluate and administer. It is most effective when it promotes the active involvement of pupils and parents as partners in the learning process.

An IEP will set targets for the child to work on in a small number of curriculum areas but does not govern the whole of the child's curriculum. Before an IEP can be devised, a baseline for the child has to be set. This is finding out exactly what the child can do rather than what he/she can not do. Once this has been established, it is easier to see more clearly what the child needs to work on.

An IEP should be SMART (Specific, Measurable, Achievable, Relevant and Time-limited):

- *Specific* – it must relate to the child's individual needs and should not cover the whole curriculum. The targets need to be very specific.
- *Measurable* – targets should have criteria for success so that everyone knows when success has been reached.
- *Achievable* – there should be small, graded steps in order to ensure success and build on what the child can already do.
- *Relevant* – they should relate to child's individual needs. It is important to find the child's baseline.
- *Time-limited* – they need to be worked on regularly and frequently. A review date must be set (either every two to five weeks or termly).

Parental involvement in their child's IEP is vital. Parents have the right to be informed about and involved in the decision-making process regarding their child. The need to review IEPs on a regular basis means that parents can be kept informed as part of an ongoing process rather than on a 'crisis-basis'.

The use of weekly or monthly evaluation notes will demonstrate progression and provide information to summarize progress for the IEP. However, the periods of these evaluation times are dependent on the needs of the school and the child and can be weekly, fortnightly, monthly or half-termly. A possible IEP/Targets Evaluation Notes format can be found on p.161. It may be advisable to place them on A3 paper.

Age-appropriate activities

An important consideration when planning objectives and activities for children is to make them age-appropriate. They need to be relevant and functional in helping to develop life skills. It is also important to consider what a child of that age would naturally be involved in and be motivated by. Age-appropriate activities need to consider the developmental stage and physical skills of the child, but fine-tuning these to fit with what his peer group is doing is not always an easy task.

Inclusion provides a more resourceful environment in which to create age-appropriate activities. Often a child's own peers come up with ideas and will travel down roads of which adults are unaware. Adults may have some awareness of youth cultures (pop groups, fashion styles and so on) as they may have children of their own, but they cannot replace peer socialization and should not really need to do so.

4 Resources

Resources Library

Providing and making adequate resources is an essential task which underpins all curriculum work. Teachers working in isolation to produce differentiated materials is time consuming and limiting. However, if a school resources library is available, then all staff can work together to acquire a network of high-quality resources. This will reduce the amount of time required to make resources (and money) and it will provide a greater breadth of resources available. It is important that staff are employed to develop these resources for colleagues and pupils, and are coordinated by a named person with a high level of expertise and skills in this area. The resources can be organized using a curriculum storage box system.

Curriculum Storage Boxes

This is a way of managing and storing resources under a specific label and subject. All resources are sorted by subject, so that when that theme or topic is taught elsewhere in the school, they are able to access appropriate resources (see p.191).

5 Partnerships

A) Professional partnerships

Working in teams

The importance of working closely together and within effective teams in all aspects of the child's life is crucial if children are to be successful and empowered. It is in this way that the team is able to draw on everyone's skills and strengths for the benefit of the child. Working together promotes ownership. Working with others is less stressful than working alone. Working in a team promotes individual competencies and growth. However, it is important to remember that in any team situation, everyone should understand and agree their roles and responsibilities.

8

Staff Network Groups

These are sessions that meet on a month or termly basis to discuss support mechanisms for pupils. They provide the staff with new ideas and an opportunity to share information. They also provide support to less experienced members of staff who require advice and encouragement.

Multi-agency work

Working with other professionals such as physiotherapists, specialist teachers and speech therapists to share advice and information is very important. How this information is shared and dessiminated from these agencies to school staff is vital. These professionals need to attend review meetings and their advice needs to be incorporated into programmes.

B) Peer Partnerships

There are a number of schemes to promote peer partnerships. They include Circle of Friends – playground friends and buddy systems (peer supporters who help in the classroom).

Circle of Friends (sometimes known as 'Circle of Support')

This is an important inclusive education tool. It provides an effective framework of peer support for children who are multiple disabled. It works by establishing a group of peers who volunteer to support the child in situations that they find difficult, and has been shown to greatly benefit children who are multiple disabled, as well as their peers.

This approach promotes the inclusion of children who often are isolated by their disability, behaviour or difference. It aims to increase the level of acceptance of the child; it provides opportunities by the child's peer group to be positively involved in the child's life, and it provides the child with a wider group of friends and range of choices. More importantly, it widens the support team to the child's peer group. There are five essential steps:

- *Preparation and planning* – it is important that the school management team are committed to this approach and that the key staff are given time to support it (generally 30 minutes per week). It is also important that the parents and the child are supportive.

- *Working with the pupils in the class* – this is a session to discuss the support of the child involving what they like about him; what they find difficult; completion of a friendship circle diagram; elicitation of empathetic feeling in the group (i.e. what makes you feel lonely, unhappy, bored and sad); and writing a list of ways to help the child (i.e. being friendly, welcoming him in the morning, inviting him to play).

- *Create a Circle of Friends* – this involves the enrolment of supporters in the class of between six to eight members.

- *Initial circle meeting* – this will discuss ways the peer support group will help and include the pupil and members take specific responsibilities (i.e. lunch-and break-time rota, club support).
- *Holding regular meetings* – these could be every week or two weeks and their purpose is to review support, their successes and failures and consider ways forward. These meetings could be chaired by the class teacher or by a responsible peer with a list of questions to ask. An important aspect is that the group members could take it in turn to entertain the child in their own home or be open to receive an invite by the child to their home.

The process increases self-confidence and esteem for both parties and it has been found that many of the relationships that have been established have continued beyond the school boundaries, extending into home situations and going on into adult life. The Circle of Friends seeks solutions to problems in an attempt to reduce difficulties and to support their friend, the child.

These circles should not exclude other children with difficulties who volunteer, as they can learn to face their own problems and difficulties through their involvement.

C) Parent partnerships

Partnerships with parents are very important. Parents probably know their child better than anybody else and, therefore, the information they hold is key to pupil achievment and progression. Communication with parents can come through formal progress and review meetings (i.e. annual reviews and parent evenings), home visits, telephone conversations or by home – school books.

Home–school books

A home–school book is a communication book between the parents of the child and the school that is written in by both parties to inform each other of events and activities taking place in school and the home. It will provide a useful dialogue of information for communication with the pupil to reinforce the past, present and the future. It will also provide a true record of events. This is particularly important if the child is prone to extend the truth about his home or school life. It will also allow the home and school to raise small issues or concerns (i.e. hospital appointments). Complex issues should be raised directly with the school or parents by telephone or formal meetings.

In the book there will need to be a copy of the pupil's timetable. Staff at school should then make daily comments on the day's activities. Full sentences are not necessary, although key points need to be emphasized. In some ways, the comments will reflect a text message (i.e. maths – telling the time – o'clock). It is important that the home – school book is used on a daily basis to initiate a conversation with the child when they come to school or return home.(i.e. 'What did you do last night?' or 'What did you do in school today?').

8

The home–school book can also be used for homework details. In secondary schools a school diary system may operate. However, this may be inappropriate in some cases, so it may be necessary to operate both systems, to gain the benefits of them.

6 School arrangements

Formulating a policy

In formulating policies it is essential that professionals explicitly address children who are multiple disabled. They need to offer a framework for developing a system in which comprehensive assessments are routine and which ensures the collection and dissemination of relevant and valid information. Policies need to integrate training into their strategic planning and discuss how communication can best be promoted across different professionals and agencies.

A school policy should ensure the following:

1 All parents should feel that their children will be welcomed and appropriately supported.

2 All staff should be committed to inclusion.

3 An inclusion policy must be an integral part of the ethos of the school and its development plan.

4 The contribution of all pupils is valued.

5 High expectations are set for all pupils.

6 Staff are trained and equipped to teach all children.

This type of school policy will help continue the good work of staff when they leave and will help to overcome the shortage of available teaching skills.

What schools will need

It is important that when new staff join the school they are briefed about pupils and programmes before working with them. At interview and transition periods, new staff need to be made aware of the necessary demands of working with a child of multiple disabilities (i.e. time for planning and making resources). Do staff have specialist training about strategies and resources required?

Schools will need:

● The support of the governing body, management and all staff.
● Staff with a knowledge and understanding of the needs of children with multiple disabilities.
● The availability of specialist advice to support both staff and pupils.
● Staff who are committed to working together with other professionals (as members of a team). They need to be allocated

additional quality time on a weekly basis to facilitate liaison and work on the child's individual programme. Staff cannot be expected to incorporate this work into their normal day.

- A willingness to change school policies and classroom practice to incorporate children, and to involve staff and peers in the ethos of accepting and supporting this group.
- To provide an appropriate curriculum alongside the National Curriculum and develop effective strategies that facilitate access to learning.
- To develop a variety of teaching and learning styles and to modify/adapt the indoor and outdoor environments to meet the child's physical and sensory needs.
- To incorporate the support and services of other qualified professionals.
- To demonstrate a commitment to in-service training, in order to increase knowledge and understanding in meeting the needs of these children.

Curriculum delivery

In order to deliver and facilitate an effective curriculum for children with multiple disabilities, adequate support arrangements will need to be in place. However, the delivery will require a focused approach, it will need to be fun and exciting, planned, well-supported and resourced, interactive, age-appropriate and be based on assessment.

Classroom arrangements

When considering the inclusion of a child with multiple disabilities a number of considerations will need to be made. The seating arrangements will need to be such that the pupils needs are paramount. For example, if the child uses a wheelchair it is important that the classroom is big enough and that he can freely move around the classroom environment and is not restricted to specific areas. It is important that careful thought is given regarding the management of support staff, where they can sit and work and that there are not too many adults in the class at the same time; the location of a visual timetable; whether a designated area needs to be allocated to the child for their personal space; and finally where equipment can be stored.

Part-time inclusion placements

These are placements when pupils spend the majority of their time in a special school, but spend a short period of time in a mainstream school (i.e. an afternoon a week). These arrangements are seldom successful, especially if they are not appropriately resourced. However, these can be successful if the following steps are taken:
- The mainstream teacher and support teacher spend time together planning the placement, outlining its programme, aims, objectives and activities.
- Appropriate staff have specialist knowledge of children with multiple disabilities and know the activities and resources required for the placement to be successful.
- Peer friendships are actively pursued through peer partnership programmes and contacts.

- Planning has taken place and resources have been provided to facilitate inclusion.

Part-time inclusion is doomed to failure without the above. Taking the child or 'turning up' does not constitute inclusion. However, this is what often happens, with inappropriate activities, inadequate planning and a lack of peer relationships. Sometimes inclusion takes place because of legal recommendations. However, if the intention is not appropriately supported, then more harm than good will result. For part time placements it is essential that staff are proven practitioners in facilitating inclusion. Without these creditials, they will be unable to establish appropriate arrangements and put things right when they go wrong.

7 Training

Staff development is a very effective way of engaging in a mutual process of change for staff, pupils and management. The importance of extending training to all is essential in facilitating inclusion. Training needs to be available not only to teachers but also to all those who are coming into contact with the child (e.g. learning support assistants, cleaners, bus escorts).

Training will need to include:

- awareness of disability
- what inclusion is and how the school should be organized to support it
- the roles of staff
- principles of working with children who are multiple disabled the selection of appropriate communication systems
- incorporating a multi-sensory curriculum
- adapting materials and the environment and
- implementing IEPs.

8 Evaluation

The process of evaluation must always be key to pupil progression and achievement. At each support framework stage this will need to be considered, however, evaluation of teaching, targets and programmes should take place at regular periods, such as reviews, parent evenings and planning sessions. The cycle of evaluation must always be linked back to assessment of need, planning and future work.

Basic principles of working with multiple-disabled children

- It is important to employ TAs as intervenors or key workers who are able to formulate a close rapport and relationship with the child, who can adopt an interactive approach enabling the child to build relationships on their own terms.

● Consistent routines which enable pupils to anticipate events are essential and there should be a consistent approach by staff towards pupils.

● It is advisable to restrict the number of support workers to each child. The more there are, the greater the communication will need to be with each other and the more likely it is for the child to be confused.

● Organized frameworks to facilitate inclusion, access to the National Curriculum and the implementation of IEPs will need to be established. Learning will need to be carefully planned in advance to adapt materials and differentiate work.

● Learning contexts will need to be multi-sensory and based on concrete experiences and activities.

● Developing communication skills will require careful planning, taking account of the child's appropriate communication mode and investigating ways of taking the child further.

● The child should have the opportunity to influence and control activities in a positive way. This can be established through letting him make choices, dictate the pace or length of an activity, or by letting him initiate something he wants to do (e.g. by using switch technology).

● Realistic objectives, IEPs and activities will need to be established.

● A peer support mechanism needs to be available (i.e. buddying and Circle of Friends).

● Environmental alterations and space for equipment need to be considered.

Aitken and Buultjens (1992) identified ten working principles or commandments in working with children who are multiple disabled.

They are:

1 Thou shalt share the learner's perspective.

2 Thou shalt open thine eyes.

3 Thou shalt ascertain strengths and abilities.

4 Thou shalt follow the learner's lead.

5 Thou shalt not compartmentalize.

6 Thou shalt adopt a united approach.

7 Thou shalt think for tomorrow.

8 Thou shalt value the learner.

9 Thou shalt give the learner time.

10 Thou shalt evaluate thine own work – not the learner.

Key points

- Legislation promotes inclusive education and equal opportunities for all pupils as a basic right. If inclusion is to be successful, local authorities will need to be highly committed to this cause.
- Inclusion requires the support of the school's senior management to facilitate policies and strategies, and to provide time for planning for these children.
- Appropriate and sufficient resources must be available to support inclusion.
- School buildings will need to be adapted to accommodate children who are multiple disabled; this is much more than just providing ramps and widening doors.
- Specialist staff will be needed, as will a commitment to staff development and training.
- Appropriate support frameworks will need to be in place to ensure the smooth running of the school and to meet the individual needs of these children.
- Schools will need to ensure that all staff, peers and school governors are aware of the basic needs of pupils who are multiple disabled, and the principles of their education.
- Realistic and appropriate IEPs will need to be established to facilitate pupil progression and progress.
- Schools will need to promote positive peer-support programmes.
- All departments within local authorities will need to work together to plan for successful inclusion.
- Local authorities will need to support a vigorous early years programme in order to provide all children with the best possible start to their education.

8

Supporting Children

9 | Access to a curriculum in mainstream education

Michael is 13 years old and has Down's Syndrome. He has normal vision and hearing but has visual perceptual difficulties. He attends a mainstream school with support. Michael has a left-sided orientation and writes with his left hand. This hand preference has only recently been confirmed and approaches are being implemented to make the appropriate adjustments for his left-hand orientation by turning the paper at a 45-degree angle and keeping his elbow straight. His visual perceptual difficulties are being overcome for writing using bold-lined paper and pens with a triangular grip. He is well accepted by his peers and has a number of special friends. He particularly enjoys learning about a broad range of curriculum areas and the resources these subjects offer.

The principle of entitlement to a broad and balanced curriculum for all pupils (and this includes those children who are multiple disabled) is fundamental to the spirit of the National Curriculum. Teachers have the flexibility to plan their own schemes of work appropriate to the needs of all the pupils in their classroom and the statements of attainment allow the teacher scope for interpretation. Fundamentally, if appropriate schemes of work and carefully structured tasks are chosen at the outset, then access to the National Curriculum will be maximized for children who are multiple disabled.

A curriculum for children with multiple disabilities needs to encompass a curriculum that meets the holistic needs of the child. For this child it will need to include five aspects:

- the National Curriculum
- a multi-sensory approach to the curriculum
- communication and self awareness
- therapy and medical support (i.e. physiotherapy, occupational therapy, speech therapy) and
- independence and Life Skills (i.e. personal, social and health education).

Previous chapters have identified the importance of a multi-sensory approach in relation to a curriculum, communication and therapy support. This chapter will focus on the National Curriculum and independence and life skills.

Ways to guide good practice

Preparation

Careful planning is essential to ensure access to the Curriculum for all. The following points are important to consider when preparing for lessons:

- Teachers will need to give support staff work in advance, so that they will have sufficient time to devise and differentiate materials.
- It is important not to limit the range of experiences offered on the assumption that some may be beyond pupils' understanding.
- Collaborative work with peers is especially important when planning activities. It is essential that children who are multiple disabled are able to play a full role and not be left out.
- Children will need more time to complete a task and repetition is essential if they are to gain a concrete and meaningful understanding of that task.
- Additional time needs to be available to prepare pupils for a task (e.g. seating, positioning, mobility restrictions).
- Additional time will be required to set up equipment or adapt materials (e.g. use of tactile pictures).

Oral presentation and delivery

The way in which the teacher or adult verbally presents lessons affects the way children access the subject. The following points are guidelines on oral presentation and delivery:

- It is important to use clear and specific instructions.
- The pupil may need to have tasks explained in a slow and deliberate way, with both verbal and physical explanations.
- Teachers will need to give detailed verbal descriptions and explanations for all information.
- The appropriate level of language and vocabulary should be used at all times.
- Oral presentation should be made interesting by varying pitch, tone and rate of speech.
- All pupils should be addressed by their name.
- All pupils should be encouraged to actively support the child who is multiple disabled by interpreting events verbally for him.
- Alternative ways to convey gestures and facial expressions need to be sought to cue, reward and praise children.
- Pupils should be given as many first-hand experiences as possible, by taking them to things and bringing things to them.

Aids to reading and writing

Pencils and crayons should be avoided as they provide less contrast than pens. However, if pens cannot be used, non-smudge crayons and a thick B-grade pencil provide better contrast than HB pencils. (Children may feel 'singled out' if they are using different materials, which is detrimental to the ethos of inclusion.) The Berol pen range is particularly good. For example, the black or red fine felt-tip is useful for providing a good model for the child to copy or to outline pictures. Children can also write with them or use the broad felt-tip pen. Felt-tip pens with a triangular grip are also available in blue and black in the Hand Hugger range. Water-based handwriting pens are also available in the Berol range and are especially helpful when they are combined with the special ink erasers. These ink erasers can also be used with the blue Hand Huggers.

There are a wide variety of holders, grips and straps available to assist children in holding a pencil or pen as seen below. Using different types of paper can be beneficial. We cannot assume that all children prefer white paper with faint lines.

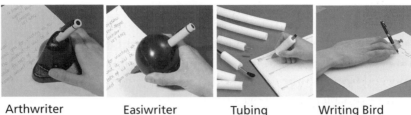

Arthwriter   Easiwriter   Tubing   Writing Bird

Triangular Grips   Finger Yoke   Ring Pen

There are a wide variety of papers available and they include:

- coloured paper
- black, wide and narrow, bold-lined paper
- black, wide and narrow, bold-lined squared paper
- red or green lined paper
- scented paper that can be scratched to reveal a smell that can then be used to distinguish tasks and activities.

Other aids that may facilitate writing and reading include the use of a sloping board, CCTV, tape recorders, large-print materials, low-vision aids (LVAs) such as magnifiers and ICT equipment.

Presenting written and reading material

When presenting worksheets and text the following points should be considered:

- Use bold typescript in black or red ink.
- Large print (18 point and above) should be used.
- Choose a paper colour which will contrast with black ink.
- Watch the quality of duplication – use the original if possible.
- Avoid plastic-covered worksheets as they reflect light and cause dazzle.
- Textbooks and worksheets should be adapted and modified and content may need to be simplified.
- The use of transparent coloured overlays may help text definition and reduce overcrowding effects.
- To colour code and box key words and information often facilitates learning.
- Avoid overcrowding by reducing the number of words on the page and by using an overcrowding frame reducer.
- Outline and simplify pictures and drawings.

Tactile pictures and diagrams

In some circumstances it may be necessary to produce tactile or raised pictures using embossing equipment, a device that converts two-dimensional drawings into tactile images, or by using junk tactile materials.

Useful embossing equipment available from the RNIB includes Hi Mark, spur wheels and German film. Hi Mark liquid can be squeezed from its tube directly onto surfaces, drying within minutes to provide a tactile marker. This is particularly useful for science beakers and cooker dials. A spur wheel produces a variety of embossed, ridged or patterned lines and can be useful for simple geometrical drawings. German film is a thin plastic sheet which is placed on a rubber mat. Lines can then be embossed on the film with a Biro. This material provides an immediate tactile result and is simple to use.

A Zy-Fuse produces raised images from two-dimensional drawings and costs around £350. It uses special microcapsule paper, which is coated with alcohol that expands when heated. The device acts like a cooker and when the paper is run through it, black areas or patterns on a white background are raised. The microcapsule paper can be purchased from Zychem Limited (see Useful Addresses on page 202) and is available in A3, A4 and B4 sizes. The cost of each picture is about  40p. This method is relatively easy and quick to use and is suitable for maps and detailed diagrams, as well as simple line drawings. Using a thick pencil or a special pen, drawings can be made directly on the special paper. Alternatively, drawings can be photocopied onto the paper.

Pictures made from junk materials provide another tactile method. Solder wire or cord can be used for line drawings, and different grades of sandpaper, crepe paper or wallpapers can create various textures. Different reliefs can be created by sticking layers of a flat material onto the base sheeting, using either card or vinyl floor tiles. It is important to always use a strong glue for sticking materials (e.g. Dunlop Thixofix, Copydex or PVA adhesive). Making these materials, however, tends to be very time consuming and costly, considering how long they are actually used by the children.

Another method of producing tactile pictures is by thermoform. This device uses junk material as a mould, which is then covered by sheet plastic that becomes the tactile picture once it has been heated. This tends to be very expensive, but it is durable and best produced by

9

Supporting Children

specialist manufacturers. The Living Paintings Trust produces famous paintings in this way and they are available for loan.

Practical tips
- Decide what kind of tactile picture is required.
- Produce a drawing of the proposed tactile picture.
- Provide a key for locating the symbols at the bottom of the page.
- Tactile pictures should be simple and uncluttered.
- They need to be clearly laid out and presented.
- Make sure they are a size that the pupil is able to scan and feel.
- They should be clearly labelled.

Board work

When writing on the board the following points need to be considered:

- Written work should be clearly and simply presented.
- Colour-code and box key words and information.
- Use white or red chalk for blackboards, red or black markers for white boards.
- Be careful of smudge marks.
- Pupils may benefit from having their own copy of board notes.
- Pupils may need to be close to the board (within one to two metres).
- Children will need to sit where visual aids can be viewed and handled.
- Children need to sit in a well-lit but glare-free position.
- Blackboards require regular maintenance and may need to be resurfaced, or sanded and painted with the correct paint.

Marking work

The pen for marking must be of a different colour from that which the pupil has used. It is recommended that red is used for marking when print is black, and when print is coloured, use black or blue ink instead.

Teacher position

When considering the position of the teacher in relation to the child the following points are important:

- Stand in the best possible position so that pupils can observe your gestures.
- Avoid standing in front of a window, as your facial features will be in shadow and they will be difficult to distinguish.
- When demonstrating a practical skill, stand behind the pupil, or slightly to the left side, with your hands in front of the child, so that he can see them in the position from which he is copying. The child's hands may need to be guided.

Furniture

Furniture should be at the appropriate height for children whether they are standing or sitting in wheelchairs or adaptive chairs. A wide range of adjustable furniture is available, including computer trolleys, tables with tilting tops, sinks, hobs and cupboards. This furniture can be adjusted by turning handles, adjusting the legs and by using an electronic lifting device. A well-known outlet for adjustable furniture is Vari-tech.

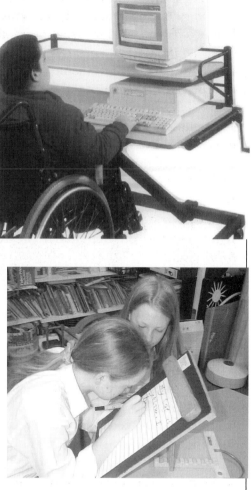

Sloping boards

A sloping board or tilted workstand may be beneficial to assist children to read and write. These should be placed in a position that is well lit, without shadow or reflection and should be covered with sheet metal and a non-slip material (e.g. dycem). Fridge magnets or magnetic guide rails are helpful to hold up work. For reading, the board should be fully raised and for writing it should be in the first position. The guide rail should be at the bottom of the board for most tasks, especially reading a book.

Transparent, coloured overlays

It has been found that the use of transparent overlays can help up to 20 per cent of children to read more easily and quickly. This applies to all children, whether they are visually impaired or not. Overlays tend to make the text clearer and more comfortable to read. They help to sort and distinguish letters within words in a very distinctive way. Children say that 'the letters don't jump around' or 'they don't fall off the page' or 'they don't fizz'.

There is no one particular colour that will work for every child. Children can choose from a range of ten colours to discover which one suits them best. If used in combination, the overlays will make up to 29 colours. Transparent, coloured overlays are available from JAG Enterprises.

Crowding frame reducer

This is a card measuring 19.5cm × 10cm with an oblong block measuring 18cm × 8cm cut out from its middle. These are approximate measurements and can be altered as required by the child and the task. This is a simple piece of equipment which reduces the effect of viewing a whole page of text, minimizing scanning skills and visual distraction by drawing attention to a narrow and specific area.

Supporting Children

Once the person has read the text inside the frame, it can then be moved to the next specified area. This equipment has provided much help to those who have visual perception difficulties and the visually impaired. Another name for a crowded frame is a Typerscope.

Eating equipment

There is a variety of cutlery and equipment available to assist people who are multiple disabled to feed themselves independently. Many of these items can be purchased from companies such as Nottingham Rehab.

They include:

Handgrips   Sculptured handled cutlery   Plate surrounds   Angled cups

Miscellaneous equipment

There is a wide range of small items that can be beneficial to children with multiple disabilities.

This includes:

- Velcro and small clamps to fix items to work surfaces
- tilted sloping boards
- cutting boards with spikes to hold vegetables
- ridged plates or boards to keep food items secure
- chisel and nail guides
- non-slip dycem mats to keep objects and body parts in position
- easigrip scissors and dual-control training scissors.

Independence and life-skills training

It is important, as part of a broad and balanced curriculum, that children with multiple disabilities leave education with skills which will equip them for life. Therefore, it is vital that life skills are taught to these children that will enable them to live independent lives. This programme of activities can be incorporated into the National Curriculum, but will need clear direction and focus, as many children with multiple disabilities do not learn these skills naturally, but require teaching and constant repetition and support. These skills will need to include the following.

Daily living skills:

- dressing and undressing
- eating and drinking
- toilet training

- cooking and preparing snacks (i.e. breakfast, sandwiches, salads, making hot and cold drinks, using a kettle and microwave)
- washing and bathing
- grooming (i.e. brushing hair, teeth, blowing nose, using deodorant/perfume)
- house-keeping (i.e. ironing, cleaning, sweeping, vacuuming, bed – making, laying the table, washing up, using a dishwasher/washing machine, scissors) and
- leisure activities (i.e. playing board games, bowling, gym, swimming, using CD, DVD player, and television).

Curriculum access:
- road safety
- using shops and leisure amenities
- using public transport
- walking to different destinations.

Davis (2001) incorporated these skills into a learning for living programme (see matrix below). She divided the skills into four life areas and then linked subjects according to their distinctive contribution to the curriculum. There are a numerous books on this subject, such as Levitt (1994) Johnson and Werner (1980), Jeffree and McConkey (1977) that can provide further guidance in this important curriculum area. The Award Scheme Development and Acreditation Network (ASDAN) is an examination body offering programmes and qualifications to develop key skills and life skills that has been extensively used in schools to facilitate this curriculum aspect.

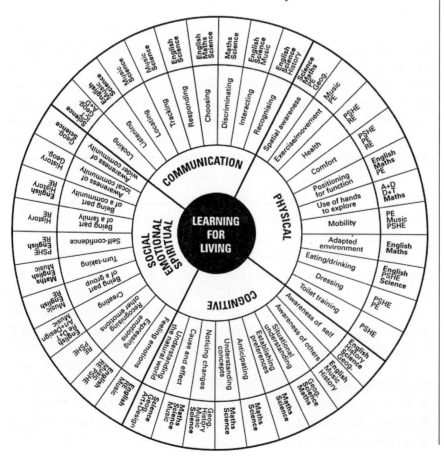

Guidlelines to facilitate subjects in the National Curriculum

English

There are four essential components to English and literacy. They are communication, listening and attending, reading, and writing. Communication has already been discussed in detail in Chapter 3. However, it must be remembered that children who are multiple disabled miss out on the incidental learning available to children without difficulties. This will invariably affect the development of communication, speech imitation and motivation to explore the world around them.

Listening and attending are major ways of gaining information and learning about the environment. Children will need to learn to habituate sounds (i.e. distinguish between essential and background sounds) and to be able to selectively choose information. This can be achieved at early stages through sound location and identification, playing with toys (play corner, water and sand), listening to songs, stories and tapes and the use of an effective intervenor.

Many children who are multiple disabled may not make connections between real-life, concrete experiences and imaginary stories, poetry and factual information. Many will require it to be sorted, translated, differentiated and organized before they can access and interpret it. They need to be encouraged to move from intentional signals to encoding symbols (i.e. words, pictures).

Reading is often exclusively concerned with the reading of words in books. However, reading goes far beyond this limited preoccupation. Some children may not reach the formal stage of reading words, but are able to read images for social meaning. However, if our viewpoint is extended regarding what is considered to be reading, and if we widen our understanding of what are considered to be books, then the world of reading and literacy is enhanced for multiple-disabled children. Within this widening viewpoint we need to include the understanding of images, signs, pictures and logos. If we do this, then the school library will become a very different place.

This library will contain a number of objects and artefacts that previously would not be considered 'reading material'. The items which would constitute 'home-made books' may include:

- interesting objects (e.g. historical artefacts and general items)
- logo materials (e.g. restaurant chain objects, football team scarves and hats)
- posters/towels (e.g. pop groups)
- bag/purse/books with objects inside them to tell a story
- picture books without words
- pop-up/three-dimensional books

9

- flick books
- table mats and coasters
- interactive books (known as story sacks or bag books)
- books with objects and
- taped stories.

Many children are able to make significant marks that they interpret as having meaning

Interactive books are books that come alive by the interaction of others. They provide opportunities for multi-sensory storytelling using story props, real objects and access technology (i.e. switches) that can be made accessible to the whole class. Most books can be made into a Bag Book. To make a book the adult needs to select appropriate props to depict the topic themes or picture (e.g. bell for door bell). Then activities need to be planned to reinforce the concepts, key words and characters of the story. Story books which have one or two lines of repeated text are great fun and add an extra dimention to the story (i.e. 'But they couldn't pull up the enormous turnip'). A Big Mac switch can be used for this purpose as the child's voice, if he has speech difficulties. Sound tapes and glove puppets can also be helpful in making stories interactive. Bag Books can be homemade or be purchased from Bag Books Limited or REACH.

For some children who are multiple disabled, the ability to write using words will be unobtainable. However, many children are able to make significant marks that they interpret as having meaning. Adults are not always able to understand or attach meaning to these marks, but should accept that these marks or drawings clearly convey meaning and feelings.

Alternative methods and materials for writing could include the use of the following:

- ultraviolet pens/paints
- pasta
- dough
- einger paint
- plasticine
- shaving foam
- washing-up liquid
- flour (wet/dry)
- sand (wet/dry)
- printing stamps
- signature stamp made by the child
- magnetic letters
- simple sentence makers
- symbol programmes (i.e. Inclusive Writer, Boardmaker, Writing with Symbols).

The National Literacy Strategy and the Literacy Hour

The Literacy Hour is for everyone. The principle of inclusion is to hold everyone's interest at a pace at which all can contribute and learn. This activity is one that all children with special needs can access, as the teaching is very explicit and structured. It provides opportunities for children to work at their own level. The teaching style is lively and interactive and suits children who have difficulties with concentration. Learning is made in the context of real events and life experiences.

For children who are multiple disabled, access to the Literacy Hour requires much preparation and forward planning. However, using a multi-sensory and tactile base, access is realistic and possible. Planning of activities needs to be considered across the whole structure of the hour and sufficient time needs to be available in advance to cooperatively plan learning materials and teaching methods. Adapting materials can be a complex process; therefore support staff need sufficient time to prepare the materials. Large print, Braille, Moon or Makaton symbols, talking books and tactile books will need to be prepared before the lesson. Some tactile stories are commercially available (e.g. from Bag Books) and are suitable materials for the Literacy Hour.

Use of tape recorders, Braillers, collecting objects or dictation to an amanuensis may need to be used for recording purposes as appropriate alternatives to handwriting.

Practical tips

Whole-class shared reading time (15 minutes)

- The child sits on the floor using a floor corner seat alongside his peers.
- Depending on his level of vision and arousal, he will sit supported or unsupported by his Intervenor.
- He may require his own copy of the big book.
- The big book may require adaption, including a tactile base and well-contrasted pictures.
- The child may need to sit to the side with the Intervenor next to him to help sort and reinforce visual and verbal information.
- Check lighting conditions.
- Use real objects to illustrate the story.
- Give clear verbal instructions.
- Present bold enlarged text and well-contrasted bold outlined pictures.

Whole-class shared writing (15 minutes)

- Work in pairs and small groups to listen and contribute to a piece of work.
- The activity will need to be differentiated.
- Use multi-sensory equipment and materials.
- Use a closed-circuit television.
- Use good quality marker pens on whiteboards (especially black and red).
- Box key words in red or a bight colour.
- Ensure that the intervenor speaks what the teacher writes on the board.
- Provide an individual whiteboard if necessary as a copy or adaption to the main board.

Group and independent work (20 minutes)
- Guided reading and writing with an intervenor and children of similar abilities.
- Reinforce work by a variety of communication modes (e.g. objects of reference).
- Introduce, reinforce and extend word vocabulary.
- Listen to the story again on tape.
- Use objects of reference to record the underlying ideas of the story.
- Use a closed-circuit television.
- Use of multi-sensory equipment and materials.
- Provide text in appropriate bold print or tactile medium.
- Provide tape recorders.
- Encourage the use of computers or other access technology equipment.

Whole-class plenary (10 minutes)
- An opportunity to re-emphasize teaching points.
- Share their work with other children.
- Practise new concepts and skills learnt.
- Actively involve the children in any demonstrations.
- Give clear verbal interpretation of discussions.

Mathematics

Numeracy is a life skill that enables a person to think and use mathematics in real-life functional situations. For many people, numeracy is used in a very basic and functional way, such as knowing the time and purchasing shopping items or travelling tickets. These tasks are usually supported by others (e.g. cashiers), who are ready to assist in accomplishing these life skills. Mathematics is important in developing communication, understanding relationships and helping the child in becoming systematic.

Children who are multiple disabled are able to access this subject if it relates to concrete examples, and if concepts are emphasized and related to everyday life. Handling, feeling edges of coins and surfaces and using money in real situations, applying time to real events and time slots, feeling and sorting two-dimensional and three-dimensional shapes are practical ways to reinforce mathematical concepts. Many everyday objects and real life situations can be used in early numeracy activities (i.e. matching items – knife and fork, counting real objects, comparing size and quantity).

Numeracy focuses on a number of themes that are often shared with and inter-related to other subjects. These include: weight; shape; texture; temperature; comparing; ordering; sequencing; sorting; volume; matching; patterns; space; time; measurement; predicting; one-to-one correspondence; counting; routines; adding (concept of 'more'); division (concept of 'sharing'); subtracting (concept of 'less'); problem-solving (cause and effect); and object permanence.

9

A wide range of equipment facilitates access to this subject:

- tactile and colourful equipment – contrasted rulers, protractors and compasses
- talking clock
- large abacus
- tactile dice
- tactile clock and large digit clockface
- stencils/templates
- dienes apparatus
- real objects for sorting and counting
- handling real money
- talking calculators
- spinners
- large three print number line and number squares
- real money
- visual timetables
- clicker software.

The National Numeracy Strategy

This strategy provides a framework for understanding and teaching numeracy at appropriate ages. It focuses on mental and written computation, solving problems and a practical understanding of graphs, diagrams, charts and tables. A typical daily lesson of 45–60 minutes is to be organized as below. Positioning children in a 'U' shape and near to the teacher helps children to feel more included and less on the edge of activities.

Practical tips

Oral work and mental computation (5–10 minutes)
- This can take place within the whole class or in small groups.
- These sessions can be reinforced by practising skills in other informal sessions.
- The intervenor can provide additional cues and reinforcement during this time.
- Oral work can be reinforced by concrete objects.

Main teaching activity (30–40 minutes)
- This part of the lesson can take place as a whole class, in groups or pairs, or on an individual basis.
- Pupils can listen and contribute to a piece of work.
- The activity will need to be differentiated.
- Use multi-sensory equipment and materials.
- Use a closed-circuit television.
- Box key words in red or a bight colour.
- Provide an individual whiteboard if necessary as a copy or adaption to the main board.

Whole-class plenary (10–15 minutes)
- An opportunity to re-emphasize teaching points.
- Share their work with other children.

9

- Practise new concepts and skills learnt.
- Actively involve the children in any demonstrations,
- Give clear verbal interpretation of discussions.

Science

It is likely there are many gaps in the pupil's learning and experience, which should not be confused with a lack of ability. Pupils may not know about subjects such as the sun, parts of the body or plants, and because of this some concepts will take longer to develop.

Demonstrations, explanations and dissection must be accessible to pupils. This may necessitate provision of individual models, specimens or equipment and close proximity to the demonstration.

The role of the intervenor, TA or support teacher to provide a commentary on what is going on is very important (e.g. experiments and their results).

Support staff will need to know in advance about practical demonstrations, in order that they can be adapted and that the pupil can be given time to become familiar with the equipment and understand how it works.

Science is a natural subject to explore and in which to develop multi-sensory experiences. The use of reactive environments can be included in a wide range of topics chosen for the mutual benefit of all children involved. Understanding how our senses work and how sensory information is integrated can also take place under the umbrella of science.

Science focuses on a number of units of work that again are often shared with and inter-related to other subjects (e.g. English and mathematics). These include: observing; predicting; hypothesising; describing; listening; looking; touching; tasting; floating; sinking; growth; materials; forces; life-cycles; body; plant and animal life. These again are aspects that occur in our everyday life and are very relevant if a multi-sensory approach is used with children who are multiply disabled.

Practical tips

- Diagrams and graphs need to have a good definition and to be well contrasted and uncluttered (containing the minimum of necessary information), and to be appropriate in size. They may need to be tactile.
- Ensure adequate support staff are available for practical work.
- Use non-slip matting (dycem).
- Use scratch-free visors which can be worn over spectacles rather than goggles.
- Use dropper bottles with pull-out spouts.
- Pour chemicals into a beaker first, then measure.
- Clamp equipment where possible to increase safety.
- Use closed-circuit television or television microscope.
- Use coloured water or food colouring for measuring.

- When lighting a bunsen burner, the pupil should be between the bunsen and tap. The adult should therefore go to the wrong side of the bench. Listen for the change in flame sound, leaving the flame blue when not in use.
- Paint the top of the bunsen burner with a contrasting colour so that pupils can see more easily where to place their taper. The use of long-handled matches may make it easier to light the burner.
- Use an adjustable table to accommodate wheelchairs and the size of pupil.
- Use alcohol thermometers as they are easier to read and are available in bright red or blue.
- Use large display digital thermometers and multi-metres.
- Provide markings on beakers using Hi-mark, Blu-tack, dymo tape and fluorescent paint.
- Plastic syringes which have been hand-calibrated with tactile markings can be used to measure acid and liquid.
- Encourage children to work in groups and to be involved in the whole activity.
- Use an audible light probe for measuring the liquid level.
- Talking thermometers, scales, voltmetres, stop watches and liquid-level indicators, calculators and scientific calculators are available to assist pupils.
- Velcro can be attached to items to fix them to surfaces.
- Cup hooks can be stuck onto items to make them easier to hold.
- Use electronic clocks and timers with large displays and control knobs for measuring time.
- Measure length with talking rulers.
- Measure weight with talking scales.
- Magnifiers and CCTV make small items (i.e. insects) more exciting to view.

Physical education and sport

Many factors may influence the participation of children who are multiple disabled in physical education (PE) activities. These factors include the appropriateness of the environment and the suitability of equipment.

It is important to check on sound quality and lighting levels in PE-teaching areas. PE lessons often take place in large, echoey halls, where the sound quality and acoustics are poor. Using soft-padded furniture and reducing the space with partitions greatly helps to improve sound quality. Using partitions will also help children who have difficulties coping with large areas of space.

Lighting should always be of good quality and should remain switched on at all times, even if it is a bright, sunny day. Even in bright sunshine, grey spots can occur, which can reduce visibility for some children. Furniture, such as benches, climbing frames and high stools, should be brightly colour-contrasted, which will clearly distinguish it from the floor and walls. Paint or coloured sticky tape can help to overcome

9

this problem. Floor markings will also need to be distinctive. This can easily be achieved by providing brightly coloured contrasting lines or by making the lines raised and tactile.

Equipment must be at an accessible height and of a reasonable size. Large equipment such as basketball, netball and badminton nets will need to be adjusted to meet the varying needs of children.

Other useful equipment includes:

● Brightly colour-contrasted bats with large handles and head.
● Brightly colour-contrasted balls with, if required, some audible quality to them (e.g. a bleeping device or beans inside them).
● Swingball – this device has a small ball attached to a cord, which is connected to a rod on a base. It is very useful for practising bat and ball skills. This equipment provides lots of opportunities to practise hitting without the inconvenience of running to fetch a ball.
● Swing football – similar to Swingball, but instead connects a football to a base and is very useful for practising kicking skills.
● Trampolines with safety handles.
● Bouncy boards to prepare children for trampoline work.
● Floatation swimming aids to support children around the neck, waist, legs and arms. A child can also be placed within a large, shaped float.
● Pollybat – a modified version of table tennis.

Playing tennis, hockey, rounders, and cricket with a large ball and bat makes these fast sports more accessible for the disabled. Pupils can also be referees or umpires for contact and team sports such as hockey, rugby and football. Another game in which all people could be involved is Goalball. In this paralympic sport, all players are blindfolded in a five-a-side arrangement to score in opposite goals, using a large ball with a bell inside.

Music

Music is an area of the curriculum that many children who are multiple disabled enjoy and are able to access easily. They can listen to and appreciate different types of musical styles and compositions. They can participate in singing songs (in whatever communication mode they select). They can play (or be helped to play) simple instruments such as bells, tambourine, drums and triangle. An instrument stand can make a secure grip for a child who is disabled to hold various instruments.

Music creates a feeling of sharing together. It can be fun. Music gives intent to the child's sounds and actions as if they are meaningful communications by the following:

● listening, watching and waiting
● making sounds to attract attention
● repeating back as in turn-taking
● responding with a different sound
● using utterances to create songs and rhythms

- make sounds to attract attention
- use loud, quiet, fast, slow, stop, start and pause.
- build up then quieten
- leave pauses for the child to respond.

An exciting music project that has recently been developed is Commusication from Soundabout. Commusication is about facilitating communication through music. A booklet, CD and DVD are available for instruction and ideas. It uses a range of interactive techniques that are enjoyable to children to enable those who are multiple disabled to enjoy music and communication through patterns of sound and silence, motivating them to develop listening and communication skills. The techniques involve the aims above, while using simple instruments, tapping of basic rhythms, repetitive chants and singing name, hello and finish songs.

Children can feel, hear and experience rhythm, pitch and intonation through using vibro-tactile beds and cushions. They will know what a bass note or a sustained note or phrase feels like through direct experience.

However, the reading and writing of musical notation and the playing of other instruments (e.g. piano, keyboard, clarinet, trumpet, flute) are not readily accessible because of the complexity of technique necessary to play them. However, Soundbeam, Midi Creator and midi-notation software can help children to access these instruments electronically.

Soundbeam is a device that emits an ultrasonic beam. When the beam is broken, the device translates these interruptions into sounds and notes through a midi-keyboard or sound module. Children with very limited mobility are able to produce high-quality sounds through this technology, which would be impossible using a conventional keyboard or musical instrument. In fact, all children, regardless of their disabilities, can benefit from using this device.

Using Soundbeam, children can discover, produce and compose good-quality music using a wide and varied bank of instruments. It encourages musical conversations, early communication skills, self-expression and mobility. It raises self-esteem and a sense of achievement, and it is great fun to use.

Through Soundbeam, children can play the chromatic, major, modal, whole tone and pentatonic scales, as well as arpeggios, and can bend and sustain notes. Soundbeam can be linked to a computer via the midi-device and therefore has the potential to produce notation of children's compositions.

The cost of this device with a sound module is around £1,800. Soundbeam can be purchased from Toys for the Handicapped and

9

a sound module is available from most specialist music shops. It is best to buy a sound module that has pads, as it can then be used as a drum or sound machine.

The Midi Creator is a similar device to the Soundbeam, except that it works on switches to produce a range of high-quality sounds. Midi Creator can be linked to a synthesizer, sound module, midi-keyboard or any device that can be controlled by an electrical domestic plug. The single switch can include any switching devices available on the market. The Midi Creator is available from Dawsons Music.

Other music projects that have proven successful include; Beat That! (Soundabout) and All Join In! (RNIB).

ICT (Information Communication Technology)

As technology continues to advance at a tremendous rate, opportunities for children with disabilities also increase. The wide range of technology available for children who are multiple disabled is both creative and varied, and provides access to the curriculum for all children.

Devices and alternatives:

- *Keyboards:* big keys, alphabetical and qwerty (KCS), concept keyboards, intellikeys, touch windows and touch screens (Inclusive Technology), keyguards.
- *Mouse:* touch pads, joysticks, trackerballs, head mouse and switches (Semerc/Resource).
- *Portable computers:* laptops, Alphasmart (Tag), DreamWriter (NTS).
- *Monitors:* large screens, touch screens, magnifying screens and screen filters, TFT, LCD monitors.
- *Scanners:* optical character recognition, such as the Robotron Rainbow (Techno-Vision Systems) and the Kurzweil (Sight and Sound).
- *CD-Rom:* access to novels, reference books, encyclopaedias, and atlases.
- *Internet:* access to talking newspapers, shopping, email and websites.
- *Interactive whiteboards:* important ICT device that can be used instead of keyboards, mice and monitors.

Other equipment:

- *Furniture:* the computer trolley needs to be adjustable so that the screen can be at eye level. This enables pupils to view the screen closely without glare. Chairs can be raised if a monitor is too high.
- *Copy-holders:* these are invaluable accessories for children as they allow text to be placed at a close distance to their eyes, leaving their hands free.

9

- *Communication boards:* Panasonic Toughbook (Centerprise), Big Mack (Liberator), Step-by-Step Communicator (Liberator), Alphatalker (Liberator), and Board Dials (Liberator).
- *Switches:* large and small jellybean switches, battery device adaptors, Universal Mounting System, Power Link, Switch Latch and Timers (SLATs), and switch interfaces (Liberator, Semerc, Rompa and TFH).
- *Tape recorders/headphones:* standard and portable.
- *Small televisions:* could be used as a monitor in conjunction with the main television.
- *Closed-circuit television:* with a colour monitor, zoom and contrast facilities. (Available from Sensory Systems and Sight and Sound, Concept Systems).
- *Talking devices:* i.e. calculators, dictionaries, scales, microwaves, talking teletext.
- *Electric scissors.*
- *Talking books/tapes.*
- *Audio-described video tapes.*

Software

There is a wide range of software available which focuses on switch operation, speech, grammar, word processing, prediction for spelling errors, screen enhancement and voice-active programmes. The table on page 190 gives some examples of companies that specialize in these particular areas.

Type	Company
Switch	Don Johnson; Semerc; Widgit; Inclusive Technology
Talking books	Sherston; Broderbund
Grammar/dyslexia	Sherston; Inclusive Technology
Word processing	Sherston; Microsoft
Symbol writing	Widgit; Inclusive Technology
Prediction	Inclusive Technology
Speech	Don Johnson; Sight and Sound; Dolphin
Screen enhancement	Sight and Sound; Dolphin
Voice active	Dragon Dictate; IBM

Art

Art is a very important means of communication for children with multiple disabilities. Art is a means of expressing ideas, which can be produced in a variety of art forms. Pupils can become skillful in using a variety of materials and tools, and are able to be creative and imaginative without the trappings of traditional perimeters. Art is the process of exploring different mediums which can then be linked to a multi-sensory approach, as well as other curriculum areas (i.e. literacy, mathematics and science).

Art ideas and equipment

- printing – use of sponges and printing stamps
- finger painting – paint can be mixed with flour, PVA glue, smells from oils, textures (i.e. rice, lentils, sand)
- marble rolling
- revolving turntable – use a lazy susan with paper cut to size and squeeze paint into the surface
- use large paint brushes, paint pads, mops and paint rollers
- rlowing paint through straws
- rubbings and etchings
- using dough and plasticine as an alternatve to clay. Add food colouring and smells from oils to increase the experience.

Curriculum boxes

In Chapter 8, I identified the importance of curriculum boxes as part of a resources library and to organizes resources to support pupils access the curriculum. The ideas below can help in developing this resource area.

Literacy box:

puppets
interactive books
magnetic letters
puzzles
logos
everyday objects
interesting artefacts
home-made books
table mats and coasters
football souvenirs
little rooms (large and small)
resonance boards
acoustic bell
ultraviolet pens
large letters
talking phot albums
puzzles
story tapes and
sound tapes.

9

Numeracy box:

number lines
threading activities
shapes
clocks
real money
rulers
talking equipment (i.e. clocks, ruler, calculator, watches)
tactile and large-embossed dice
mathematics games
accessible compass
abacus and
large-print protractor.

Science box:

magnets and non-metal objects
plastic syringes
talking devices (i.e. thermometer, scales, voltimeters, stop watch,
timers, scientific calculator)
non-slip matting
dropper bottles
light prob
liquid level indicator
sand tray with objects and containers
water tray with objects that float, sink and can be filled
clamps
velcro
mirrors
bubble-making equipment
balloons
magic sand (as soon as it comes out of water it try)
smelly cups
flavoured jelly and
coloured food flavouring.

PE box:

brightly coloured large balls and bats
sponge balls (large and small)
beanbags, brightly coloured
yellow tape for marking equipment and floor
balls with a bell/beans or sound inside
brightly colours vests
goalball equipment
pollybat
swingball
therapy ball and wedges and
large soft play equipment.

Music box:

resonance board
acoustic bell

vibro-tactile equipment
soundbeam
midi creator
different sized beaters
range of instruments (i.e. tamporines, drums, cymbals, maracas)
bracelet bells and
music tapes.

Art box:
large paint brushes
paint rollers
paint pads
revolving turntable
straws
rice, lentils, sand
dough
plasticine
sponges of different sizes and shapes
painting stamps – homemade and purchased and
variety of textures and small objects.

Key points
- A curriculum for children with multiple disabilities needs to be holistic, broad and balanced, and include the National Curriculum, therapy and medical support, independence and life skills.
- It is important to consider all materials and requirements necessary for the child to access the lesson, well in advance of that session.
- Consider reading and writing aids and how work can be presented and differentiated.
- Remember the importance of life skills, with special focus on daily living skills and curriculum access skills.
- Develop equipment and resources that will provide effective access to the curriculum, that are appropriately stored and organized in Resource Boxes.
- Make equipment which is interactive and can be used across a number of curriculum areas.
- Develop a school library that has items that all children can use and enjoy, which includes non-traditional reading materials.
- Purchase technology that will enable children to access the curriculum (i.e. talking devices, CCTV, Soundbeam, switches, alternative keyboard and mouse, software).

10 | Final thoughts

We need to endeavour to RESPECT each other as individuals and to:

Develop **R** elationships.
Show **E** mpathy for the difficulties each has to overcome.
Deal **S** enistively with each person's feelings.
Have **P** atience and wait for achievement.
Raise **E** nthusiasm with children.
Keep **C** ommunication open.
Develop **T** rust through shared experiences and being with each other.

Many children with multiple disabilities live in a state of learnt helplessness. They learn to rely on others for all their needs and to make decisions on their behalf. Many shut themselves off and enter their own internal world, where the riches within it outweigh the obstacles outside it. For them to participate in our world, these children need to be empowered, fulfilled and accepted. They need to be given the right support, understanding and resources that will equip them to lead a fulfilling life with dignity and respect. I hope that this book will equip you with the knowledge to provide the appropriate support and resources to help children with multiple disabilities. This, in turn, will facilitate their right to be included in mainstream education.

Inclusion is not about removing the child's disabilities but is concerned with placing children within environments where their disabilities are accepted and minimized, where barriers are overcome within their own local community.

The law enables the disabled. Do we?
Every child matters
Remember – Don't say 'No' but say 'Not Yet'.
Let us be champions and ambassadors of empowering and enabling children with multiple disabilities.
Now go and find the key(s) that will unlock the door for learning and change the world for that child.

Glossary

AETIOLOGY	The science of the causes of disease – a branch of medical science concerned with the causes and origins of disease.
ANOXIA	Lack of oxygen. The term usually refers to a condition caused by starvation of oxygen to a baby during a long and difficult labour.
APHASIA/APHASIC	Defect in or loss of the ability to speak or write or understand language due to brain damage.
APLASIA	Complete or partial failure of a tissue or an organ to develop.
AQUEOUS FLUID	A watery fluid in the eye that is constantly drained away and replaced. It is located behind the cornea.
ASYMMETRIC TONIC NECK REFLEX	A newborn placed on their back will assume a position with their head to one side, arms and legs on that side extended and opposite limbs flexed. It may be present at birth or may appear at about two months and disappear at about six months.
ATAXIA	Loss of coordination, though the power necessary to make the movements is still present (e.g. may have good grasp in each hand but be unable to perform fine-motor movements).
ATHETOID/ATHETOSIS	Involuntary movements affecting hands, face, tongue and feet, caused by disease to the brain.
AUDITORY	Sense of hearing.
BILATERAL	Having two sides, or pertaining to both sides.
CEREBELLUM	Part of the brain concerned with coordination of movement and maintaining equilibrium.
CEREBRAL CORTEX	The folded outer layer of the brain.
CEREBRUM	The largest part of the brain.
CONGENITAL	Refers to conditions that are present at birth.
CONJUNCTIVA	This is the outer cover of the eye and is a protective membrane. It provides lubrication and nutrients to the iris.
CORNEA	This is known as the first optic lens. It is the clear 'window' of the eye allowing light to pass through it: responsible for 60 per cent of image refraction.
DIENES APARATUS	Educational equipment comprising of wooden rods grouping cubes.
DIPLEGIA	Paralysis or stiffness of all four limbs. Legs are more affected than arms.
DIRECTIONALITY	Concerned with the spatial understanding of forward and backward motion.
DYCEM	Non-slip, rubber-like material.
DYSPLASIA	Term used to describe the difficulties in understanding language and self-expression.
DYSTROPHY	A disorder of an organ or tissue.
GASTROESOPHAGAL REFLUX	A condition where the stomach contents flow back into the oesophagus (gullet).
GASTROSTOMY TUBE	Surgical opening into the stomach from the outside to enable a feeding tube to be passed through into it.
GUSTATORY	Sense of taste.
HAPTIC PERCEPTION	Touch using the hands.
HEMI-	Prefix denoting half.
HYPERTONIA	Stiffness of the muscles.
HYPOTONIA	Floppiness of the muscles.
HYPOTONIC	Mixture of both floppiness and stiffness of the muscles.
IRIS	The coloured part of the eye containing the pupil muscles. These contract when there is a lot of light and expand when there is low light.
KINAESTHETIC	Used to describe muscle tension and position of or movement of joints and muscles.
LATERALITY	Concerned with the spatial understanding of left and right.
LENS	A soft clear capsule in the eye, which alters shape to focus images onto the retina. The lens is responsible for 40 per cent of image refraction.

LIGHT PERCEPTION	A person with light perception can see only light and colours.
MACULA	Part of the retina. It distinguishes fine detail and is the area the lens concentrates images on.
MONOPLEGIA	Paralysis or stiffness of one limb.
MORO REFLEX	The baby throws their head back and the fingers fan out. The arms then return to embrace the body and the baby cries.
MRI SCAN	Magnetic Resonance Imaging. A scan produced by a tunnel-like machine which uses a magnetic field rather than X-rays to produce excellent images of the brain, spinal cord and the organs of the pelvis. The images are viewed on a computer-controlled monitor screen.
NEO-NATAL JAUNDICE	Newborn jaundice resulting in the immaturity of the baby's liver coupled with the breakdown of the red blood cells.
OLFACTORY	Sense of smell.
ORTHOTICS	Mechanical supports for weak joints and muscles, or to correct deformity.
OSTEO	Relating to bone.
PALATE	The roof of the mouth.
PALMAR GRASP	Whole-hand grasp.
PALSY	Alternative term for paralysis.
PARAPLEGIA	Paralysis or stiffness of both legs, accompanied generally by paralysis of the bladder and rectum.
PERI	Around or near.
PINCER GRASP	Thumb and first finger grasp.
PLACING REFLEX	The baby lifts its foot and places it on a hard surface.
PLANTAR GRASP	Grasp in the foot.
PROPRIOCEPTIVE	Receptors located inside tendons, muscles and joints help us to coordinate movement and know the position of our body.
PUPIL	This is the central point of the iris. This is simply a hole that allows light and images to pass through. The hole changes in size according to the degree of light.
QUADRIPLEGIA	Paralysis or stiffness of all four limbs.
RECRUITMENT	This is an adverse reaction to loud sounds by hearing aid wearers, resulting in extreme pain and a lack of tolerance. This is remedied by calibrating hearing aids appropriately.
REFLUX	Fluid flowing in the opposite direction to normal. Often refers to regurgitation of the stomach contents into the oesophagus.
RENAL	Related to the kidneys.
RETINA	This is the area of the eye on which images are focused before they are transmitted to the optic nerve.
ROOTING REFLEX	This is when the baby turns towards an object or stimulus.
TRIPOD GRASP	Thumb and two-finger grasp.
SAVING REFLEX	Baby reacts to falling by using his hands to save himself.
SCLERA	This is the white outer coating of the eye and its function is to protect the contents of the eye.
SCOLIOSIS	Curvature of the spine.
SYNDROME	Group of symptoms occurring together to constitute a disorder.
TALIPES	Club foot, a deformity in which the foot is twisted at the ankle joint, so that the sole no longer rests on the ground.
TENDON	A band of fibrous tissue forming at the end of a muscle and attaching it to the bone, which the muscle acts on when it contracts.
THALAMUS	The centre of the brain, part of the limbic system.
TINNITUS	White or hissing noise within the ears.
TRAUMA	Injury or damage.
TRIPLEGIA	Paralysis or stiffness of three limbs.
VESTIBULAR	Located in the semi-circular canal in the ear; responsible for balance.
VITREOUS BODY	This is located behind the lens in the eye and filled with a jelly-like substance. It makes the eye feel firm and rubbery.

References

Aitkin, S. and Buultjens, M. (1992), *Assessing Functional Vision of Learners who are Multiply Disabled,* Moray House Publications.

Beat That! (1997), Soundabout.

Beukelman, D. and Mirenda, P. (1998), *Augmentative and Alternative Communication,* P Brookes Publications.

Best, A. (1992), *Teaching Children with Visual Impairment,* Open University Press.

Bidabe, L. (1992), 'Written application to the International Rotary for funding to research the MOVE programme in Australia'.

Bonar, A. (1986), *Herbs – A Complete Guide to their Cultivation and Use,* Hamlyn Publishing.

Bond, D. E. (1993), *Mental Health in Children who are Hearing Impaired in Varma,* Cassell.

Cassell, P. (1989), *The Wheelchair Child,* Souvenir Press.

Chapman, E. and Stone, M. (1988), *Special Needs in Ordinary Schools – The Visually Handicapped Child in the Classroom,* Cassell.

Contact A Family, CAF Directory.

Davis, J. (2001), *A Sensory Approach to the Curriculum,* David Fulton Publishers.

Evans, B. (2001), *Dyslexia and Vision,* Whurr.

Evans, M., Fanzen, S. and Oxenford, R. (1999), *The Massage Manual,* Hermes House.

Fox, G. (1993), *A Handbook for Special Needs Assistants,* David Fulton.

Gibson, J. and Pick, H. (1974), *Perception,* edited by R. MacLaod, Cornell University Press.

Gunzburg, H. (1973), *Social Competence and Mental Handicap,* Bailliere-Tindall.

Hewett, D. and Nind, M. (1998), *Interaction in Action – Reflections on the use of Intensive Interaction.* David Fulton Publishers.

Irlen, H. (1991), *Reading by the Colors.* Avery Publications.

Jeffree, D., McConkey, R. and Hewson, S. (1977), *Teaching the Handicapped Child,* Human Horizons Series, Souvenir Press.

Jeffree, D. and McConkey, R. (1977), *Let me Speak,* Human Horizons Series, Souvenir Press.

Johnson, V. and Werner, R. (1980), *Step-by-Step Learning Guide for Retarded Infants and Children,* Constable Publications.

Jordan, I. (1999), *Visual Dyslexia: A guide for parents and teachers,* Desktop Publications.

Jordan, I. (2003), *The Circle of Underachievement,* Desktop Publications.

Jordan, I. (2005), *How to screen for Visual Dyslexia: Visual dyspraxia and other vision-linked stress,* Desktop Publications.

Langley, B. (1986), *Sensory Impairment in Mentally Handicapped People,* edited by D. Ellis, Croom Helm.

Lee, M. and MacWilliam, L. (1995), *Movement, Gesture and Sign,* RNIB.

Lee, M. and MacWilliam, L. (2005), *Learning Together. A creative approach to learning for children with multiple disabilties and a visual impairment*, RNIB,

Levitt, S. (1994), *Basic Abilities. A developmental guide for children with Disabilities,* Human Horizon Series, Souvenir Press.

Longhorn, F. (1992), *A Sensory Curriculum for Very Special People,* Souvenir Press.

Macpherson, G. (1999), *Black's Medical Dictionary,* A & C Black.

McInnes, J. and Treffry, J. (1984), *Deafblind Infants and Children: A Developmental Guide,* Toronto Press.

Meares, O. (1980), *Figure Ground, Brightness Contrasts and Reading Disabilities,* Visible Language 14, pp. 13–29.

Millar, S. (2004), *Personal Communication Passports. Guidelines for Good Practice,* CALL Centre Edinburgh.

Mittler, P. (1987), foreword to E. Chapman, and J. Stone (1988), *Special Needs in Ordinary Schools: The Visually Handicapped Child in your Classroom,* Cassell.

Newton, C. and Wilson, D. (2003), *Creating Circles of Friends: A Peer Support and Inclusion Workbook,* Inclusion Solutions.

Nielsen, L. (1992), *Educational Approaches for Visually Impaired Children,* Sikon Publishers.

Ockelford, A. (1994), *Objects of Reference,* RNIB.

Pickles, P. (1998), *Managing the Curriculum for Children with Severe Motor Difficulties: A Practical Approach,* David Fulton Publishers.

Portwood, M. (1999), *Developmental Dyspraxia,* David Fulton Publishers.

Rikhye, C., Gothelf, C. and Appell, M. (1989), *Classroom Environmental Checklist,* St Luke's/Roosevelt Hospital Centre.

Ripley, K. , Daines, B. and Barret, J. (1977), *Dyspraxia: A guide for teachers and parents,* David Fulton Publishers.

RNIB (1990), *New Directions,* RNIB.

RNIB (1996), *All Join In* Ockleford.

Sanderson, H., Harrison, J. and Price, S. (1995), *Aromatherapy and Massage for People with Learning Difficulties,* Hands-on Publishing.

Sebba, J. and Sachdev, D. (1997), *What Works in Inclusive Education,* Barnardo's Child care Publishing.

Stillman, R. (1985), *The Calier-Azusa Scale,* South Central Regional Centre for Services to Deafblind Children.

Stordy, J. (2000), *The LCP Solution: The Remarkable Nutritional Treatment for ADHD, Dyslexia and Dyspraxia,* Ballantine Books.

Van Dijk, J. (1966), 'The First Steps of the Deafblind Child towards Language', *International Journal for the Education of the Blind,* Vol. 15, No. 4.

Warren, D. H. (1984), *Blindness and Early Childhood Development,* American Foundation for the Blind.

Winstock, A. (1994), *The Practical Management of Eating and Drinking Difficulties in Children,* Winslow Press.

Wilkins, A. (1991), *Reading through Colou,* John Wiley & Sons.

Wyman, R. (1986), *Multiply-Handicapped Children,* Souvenir Press.

Useful books

Bidabe, L. (1986), 'Written application to the International Rotary for funding to research the MOVE programme in Australia, MOVE'.

Bloom, Y.(1990), *Object Symbols: A communication option*, Monograph Series.

Bradley, H. (1991), *Assessing Communication Together*, MHNA.

Bradley, H. and Snow, R. (1994), *Making Sense of the World*, SENSE.

Cameron, R. J. (1982), *Working Together: Portage in the UK*, NFER-Nelson.

Cunningham, C. and Sloper, P. (1978), *Helping Your Handicapped Baby*, Human Horizons Series, Souvenir Press.

Coupe, J. (1985), *Affective Communication Assessment*, SERIS.

Goold, L., Borbilas, P., Clarke, A. and Kane, L. (1993), *An Ideas Kit*, North Rocks Press.

Hargreaves, J. (1986), *Cookery for Handicapped People*, Souvenir Press.

Johns, R. and Scott, L. (2001), *Let's Do it!*, Images in Action.

Johnson, V. and Werner, R. (1980), *A Step-by-Step Learning Guide for Older Retarded Children*. Constable, London.

Kerr-Edwards, L. and Scott, L. (2003), *Talking Together*. Family Planning Association.

Longhorn, F. (1993), *Planning a Multi-Sensory Massage Programme for Very Special People*, Catalyst Education.

Longhorn, F. (1994), *Sensory Science Curriculum*, Human Horizons Series, Souvenir Press.

Longhorn, F. (2000), *Numeracy for Very Special People*, Catalyst Education.

Longhorn, F. (2000), *Sex Education and Sexuality for Very Special People*. Catalyst Education.

Miles, T. R. and Miles, E. (1983), *Help for Dyslexic Children*, Routledge.

Nielson, L. (1990), *Are You Blind?*, Sikon.

Nielson, L. (1992), *Space and Self*, Sikon.

Nolan, M. and Tucker, I. (1981), *The Hearing Impaired Child and the Family*, Human Horizon Series, Souvenir Press.

Pease, L., Porter, J. and Wrench, K. (1999), *Improving Provision for Children with Muitiple Disabilities and Visual Impairment*, RNIB.

Phillips, R. and Rix, M. (1998), *Scented Plants*, Random House.

Scotson, L. (1985), *Doran: child of courage*, Pan Books.

Sienkiewicz-Mercer, R. and Kaplan, S. (1985), *I Raise my Eyes to Say 'Yes'!*, Grafton-Collins.

Smythe, I. (1999), *Dyslexia Handbook 2000*, British Dyslexia Association.

Staves, L. (2001), *Mathematics for Children with Severe and Profound Learning Difficulties*. David Fulton Publishers.

Stanton, M. (1992), *The Cerebral Palsy Handbook*, Vemilion Publications.

Wood, M. (1984), *Living with a Hyperactive Child*, Human Horizon Series Souvenir Press,.

Useful Addresses and Websites

Advisory Centre for Education (ACE) Ltd
1c Aberdeen Studios
22 Highbury Grove
Highbury
London
N5 2DQ
Tel No: 020 7704 3370 (Office)
        0808 800 5793 (Advice line)
www.ace-ed.org.uk

Afasic
2nd Floor
50–2 Great Sutton Street
London
EC1V ODJ
Tel No: 020 7490 9410 (Office)
        0845 355 5577 (Helpline)
Fax No: 020 7251 2834
Email: info@afasic.org.uk
www.afasic.org.uk

ASDAN
Wainbrook House
Huddsvale Road, St George
Bristol
BS5 7HY
Tel No: 0117 9411126
Fax No: 01179 9351112
Email No: info@asdan.co.uk
www.asdan.co.uk

Asthma UK
Summit House
70 Wilson Street
London
EC2A 2DB
Tel No: 020 7786 4900 (Office)
www.asthma.org.uk

Anything Left-Handed
18 Avenue Road
Belmont
Surrey
SM2 6JD
Tel No: 020 8770 3722
Fax No: 020 8715 1220
www.anythingleft-handed.co.uk

Association for Spina Bifida and Hydrocephalus (ASBAH)
42 Park Road
Peterborough
PE1 2UQ
Tel No: 01733 555 988
Fax No: 01733 555 985
www.asbah.org

B Squared
Unit 4C
Vulcan Close
Sandhurst
Berkshire
GU47 9DD
Tel No: 0845 4660141
www.bsquared.co.uk

Bag Books
60 Walham Grove
London
SW6 1QR
Tel/Fax No: 020 7385 4021
Email: bagbooks@appleonline.net
www.bagbooks.org

Beat That!
19 Florence Park Road
Florence Park
Oxford
OX4 3PN
Tel No: 01865 772213 /351765

BeActive Box
Suffolk Playworks
Gislingham Road
Thornham Magna
Suffolk
IP23 8HH
Tel No: 01379 788154
Email: info@playworks.co.uk
www.playworks.co.uk

Bobath Centre for Children with Cerebral Palsy
Bradbury House
250 East End Road
East Finchley
London
N2 8AU
Tel No: 020 8444 3355
Fax No: 020 8444 3399
www.bobath.co.uk

British Dyslexia Association
98 London Road
Reading
RG1 5AU
Tel No: 0118 966 8271 (Helpline)
www.bdadyslexia.org.uk

British Epilepsy Association
New Anstey House
Gate Way Drive
Yeadon
Leeds
LS19 7XY
Tel No: 0113210 8800
Fax No: 0113391 0300
Email: epilepsy@epilepsy.org.uk
www.epilepsy.org.uk

Brittle Bone Society
Grant-Paterson House
30 Guthrie Street
Dundee
DD1 5BS
Tel No: 08000 282 459 (Helpline)
Fax No: 01382 206 771
Email: bbs@brittlebone.org
www.brittlebone.org

Call Centre
University of Edinburgh
Paterson's Land
Holyroad Road
Edinburgh
EH8 8AQ
Scotland
Tel No: 0131651 6235
Email: info@callcentrescotland.org.uk
www.callcentre.education.ed.ac.uk

**Centre for Complementary and
   Integrated Medicine**
56 Bedford Place
Southampton
SO15 2DT
Tel No: 023 8033 4752
Fax No: 020 7224 4159
www.complemed.co.uk

**Centre for Studies on Inclusive
   Education (CSIE)**
New Redland
Frenchay Campus
Coldharbour Lane
Bristol
BS16 1QU
Tel No: 0117 344 4007
Fax No: 0117 344 4005
http://inclusion.uwe.ac.uk/csie/

CHARGE Association
www.widerworld.co.uk/charge

**Children's Chronic Arthritis
   Association**
www.ccaa.org.uk

**Cleft Lip and Palate Association
   (CLAPA)**
235–37 Finchley Road
London
NW3 6LS
Tel No: 020 7431 0033
www.clapa.cwc.net

Congenital CMV Association
128 Northfields Lane
Brixam
Devon
TQ5 8RH
Tel No: 01803 856496
Email: keri@brixham 128*.freeserve.
   co.uk
www.patient.co.uk

Contact a Family
209–11 City Road
London
EC1U 1JN
Tel No: 020 7608 8700 (Office)
         0808 808 3555 (Helpline)
Fax No: 020 7608 8701
Email: info@cafamily.org.uk
www.cafamily.org.uk

Coopers Healthcare
Sunrise Medical Ltd
Sunrise Business Park
High Street
Wollaston
West Midlands
DY8 4PS
Tel No: 01384 446 688
Fax No: 01384 446 699
www.sunrisemedical.co.uk

Cystic Fibrosis Trust
11 London Road
Bromley
BR1 1BY
Tel No: 020 8464 7211
Fax No: 020 8313 0472
www.cftrust.org.uk

Desktop Publications
11 Chapel Court
Brigg
DN20 8JZ
Tel No: 01652 656552
www.desktoppublications.co.uk

Diabetes UK
10 Parkway
London
NW1 7AA
Tel No: 020 7424 1000
Email: info@diabetes.org.uk
www.diabetes.org.uk

Dolphin Computer Access Ltd
Technology House
Blackpole Estate West
Worcester
WR3 8TJ
Tel No: 01905 754 577
Fax No: 01905 754 559
Email: info@dolphinuk.co.uk
www.dolphinuk.co.uk

Don Johnston Special Needs Ltd
18 Clarendon Court
Calver Road
Winwick Quay
Warrington
WA2 8QP
Tel No: 01925 256500
Fax No: 01925 241 745
Email: info@donjohnston.co.uk
www.donjohnston.co.uk

Down's Syndrome Association
Langdon Down Centre
2A Langdon Park
Teddington
TW11 9PS
Tel No: 0845 2300372
Fax No: 0845 2300373
Email: info@downs-syndrome.org.uk
www.dsa-uk.com

Dreamwriter Solutions (UK) Ltd
Portable Technology Solutions LTD
West Midlands House
Gipsey Lane
Willenhall
WV13 2HA
Tel No: 01902 482540
Fax No: 01902 482541
www.portabletechnology.co.uk

Dyscalculia.Org
8053N
Delaney Road
Henderson
M1 48841
USA
www.dyscalculia.org

Dyscalculia
Next Generation
68 Hamilton Road
Taunton
Somerset
TA1 2ES
Tel No: 01823 289559
Email: next.generation@virgin.net
www.dyscalculia.co.uk

Dyslexia Institute
Park House
Wick Road
Egham
Surrey
TW20 OHH
Tel No: 01784 222300
Fax No: 01784 222333
www.dyslexia-inst.org.uk

Dyspraxia Foundation
8 West Alley
Hitchin
SG5 1EG
Tel No: 01462 454 986
Fax No: 01462 455 052
Email: dyspraxia@dyspraxiafoundation.
    org.uk
www.dyspraxiafoundation.org.uk

Dystonia Society
89 Albert Embankment
London
SE1 7TP
Tel No: 0845 458 6322
Fax No: 0845 458 6311

Email: brianu@dystonia.org.uk
www.dystonia.org.uk

Edward Marcus Ltd
Unit 3
Marrtree Business Park
Oxspring
S36 8ZP
Tel No: 01226 764082
Email: sales@edwardmarcus.co.uk
www.mahnifier.fsnet.co.uk

Encephalitis Information Resource
7B Saville Street
Malton
YO17 7LL
Tel No: 01653 699 599
www.esg.org.uk

Education and Resources for
    Improving Childhood Continence
34 Old School House
Britannia Road
Kingswood
Bristol
BS15 8DB
Tel No: 0117 3012101
Email: info@eric.org.uk
www.eric.org.uk

Entitlement and Quality Education
    for Pupils with Severe Learning
    Difficulties (EQUALS)
www.equals.co.uk

G & S Smirthwaite Ltd
16 Wentworth Road
Heathfield
Newton Abbot
Devon
TQ12 6TL
Tel No: 01626 835 552
Email: enquiries@smirthwaite.co.uk
www.smirthwaite.co.uk

Handicom
Orangelaan 29
3843 AA Harderwijk
Netherlands
Tel NO: +31 341 412629
Email: info@handicom.nl
www.handicom.nl

Haemophilia Society
First Floor
Patersham House
57A Hatton Garden
London
EC1N 8JG
Tel No: 020 7831 1020
0800 018 6068 (Helpline)
Email: info@haemophilia.org.uk
www.haemophila.org.uk

Hemipegia
HemiHelp
Camelford House
89 Albert Embankment
London
SE1 7TP
Tel No: 0845 1203713 (Helpline)
Email: support@hemihelp.org.uk
www.hemihelp.org.uk

Health & Safety Executive
Caerphilly Business Park
Caerphilly
CF83 3GG
Tel No: 0845 345 0055
www.hse.gov.uk

Inclusive Technology Ltd
Gatehead Business Park
Delph New Road
Delph
Oldham
OL3 5BX
Tel No: 01457 819 790
Fax No: 01457 819 799
www.inclusive.co.uk

Information Exchange
1A Potters Cross
Wootton
Bedfordshire
MK43 9JG
Tel No: 0845 1275281

**International Federation of
   Aromatherapists**
61–3, Churchfield Road
London
W3 6AY
Tel No: 020 8992 9605
www.ifaroma.org

ioo Sales Ltd
56-62 Newington Causeway
London
SE1 6DS
Tel No: 020 7378 0330
www.ioosales.co.uk

JAG Enterprises
11 Glenisla View
Alyth
Blairgowrie
Perthshire
PH11 8LW
Scotland
Tel/Fax No: 01828 632679
Email: jag.enterprises@care4free.net
www.jaglowvision.co.uk

Keytools Ltd
PO Box 700
Southampton
SO17 1LQ
Tel No: 023 8058 4314
Fax No: 023 8055 6902

Email: info@keytools.com
www.keytools.com

**Lawrence-Moon-Bardet-Biedl Society
   (LMBB)**
1 Blackthorn Avenue
Southborough
Tunbridge Wells
TN4 9YA
Tel No: 01892 685311
Email: julie.sale@lmbbs.org.uk
www.lmbbs.org.uk

**Listening Programme
Unique Sounds**
17 Lancelyn Court
Wirral
CH 639JJ
Tel No: 0151 3343566
www.soundtherapy.co.uk

**Listening Programme
Advanced Brain Technologies**
5748 South Adams Avenue
Pathway
Ogden
UT 84405
Email: info@advancedbrain.com
www.advancedbrain.com

Liko (UK) Ltd
Brunel Centre
Stroudwater Business Park
Stonehouse
Gloucester
GL10 3RU
Tel No: 01453 827272
Fax No: 01453 828844
Email: info@liko.co.uk
www.liko.com

Leckey
James Leckey Design
Kilwee Business Park
Dunmurry
Belfast
Northern Ireland
BT17 OHD
Tel No: 0800 318 265
www.leckey.com

Liberator Ltd
Whitegates
Swinstead
Grantham
Lincolnshire
NG33 4PA
Tel No: 01476 550 391
Fax No: 01476 550 357
www.liberator.co.uk

Living Paintings Trust
Unit 8
Queen Isabelle House
Kingsclere Park
Newbury

RG20 4SW
Tel No: 01635 299 771
Fax No: 01635 299 771
Email: lpt@livingpaintings.org
www.livingpaintings.org

Maltron
Castlefields
Stafford
Staff
ST16 1BU
Tel No: 0845 2303265
Email: sales@maltron.co.uk
www.maltron.com

Marfan Association UK
Rochester House
5 Aldershot Road
Fleet
Hampshire
GU 51 3NG
Tel No: 01252 810 472
Fax No: 01252 810 473
www.marfan.org.uk

Makaton Vocabulary Project
31 Firwood Drive
Camerley
Surrey
GU15 3QD
Tel No: 01276 61390
Email: mvdp@makaton.org
www.makaton.org

MENCAP
123 Golden Lane
London
EC1Y ORT
Tel No: 020 7454 0454
Fax No: 020 7696 5540
Email: information@mencap. org.uk
www.mencap.org.uk

Massage in Schools
Tel No: 0777304 4282
www.massageinschools.com

Meningitis Trust
Fern House
Bath Road
Stroud
Gloucestershire
GL5 3TJ
Tel No: 01453 768 000 (Office)
Fax No: 01453 768 001
Email: info@meningitis-trust.org.uk
www.meningitis-trust.org.uk

MOVE Europe
The Disability Partnership
Wooden Spoon House
5 Dugard Way
London
SE11 4TH
Tel No: 020 7414 1493

Fax No: 020 7414 1495
Email: move@disabilitypartnership.co.uk
www.disabilitypartnership.co.uk

Multiple Disability Service
7 The Square
111 Broad Street
Edgbaston
Birmingham
B15 1AS
Tel No: 0121 643 9912

Multiple Sclerosis Resource Centre
7 Peartree Business Centre
Peartree Road
Stanway
Colchester
CO3 OJN
Tel No: 0800 783 0518
Fax No: 01206 505449
www.msrc.co.uk

Muscular Dystrophy Campaign
7–11 Prescott Place
London
SW4 6BS
Tel No: 020 7720 8055
Email: info@muscular-dystrophy.org
www.muscular-dystrophy.org

National Autistic Society
393 City Road
London
EC1 1NG
Tel No: 020 7833 2299
www.nas.org.uk

National Autistic Society (ASPEN)
9 Aspen Circle
Edison
New Jersey
08820
www.aspennj.org

National Eczema Society
Hill House
Highgate Hill
London
N19 5NA
Tel No: 0870 241 3604
Fax No: 020 7281 6395
Email: info@eczema.org.uk
www.eczema.org.uk

National Institute of Conductive Education
Cannon Hill House
Russell Road
Moseley
Birmingham
B13 8RD
Tel No: 0121 449 1569
Fax No: 0121 449 1611
Email: info@conductive-education.org.uk
www.conductive-education.org.uk

Niemann-Pick Disease Group
11 Greenwood Close
Fatfield
Washington
Tyne & Wear
NE38 8LR
Tel No: 0191 4150693
www.niemannpick.org.uk

Nottingham Rehabilitation
Victoria Business Park
Pintail Close
Netherfield
Nottingham
NG4 2PE
Tel No: 0845 121 8111
www.nrs-uk.co.uk

Orthoscopics Ltd
Kingfisher House
High Green
Great Shelford
Cambridge
CB2 5EG
Tel No: 01223 843200
www.orthoscopics.com

Osteopetrosis Support Trust
www.osteopetrosis.co.uk

PLAN (People with Leber's Amaurosis)
C/O Contact a Family
Email: chezac@marley88.fsnet.co.uk

Pivats
Lancashire County Council
PO Box 61
County Hall
Preston
Lancashire
Tel No: 01772 531525
Email: pivats@ed.lancscc.gov.uk
www.lancashire.gov.uk/education/
  pivats

PMLD Link
Carol Ouvry
31 Birdwell Road
Bristol
BS41 9BD
Tel No: 01275 394621
Email: pmld@mansell.wyenet.co.uk

**Pyramid Educational Consultants UK
  Ltd (PECS)**
Pavilion House
6 Old Steine
Brighton
BN1 1EJ
Tel No: 01273 609555
www.pecs.org.uk

Reactive Environments
3 Mulberry Court
Barking

Essex
IG11 9LQ
Email: mednick.family@tesco.net

Resource
51 High Street
Kegworth
Derbyshire
DE72 2DA
Tel No: 0870 7770247
Fax No: 01509 672 267
www.resourcekt.co.uk

REACH – National Advice Centre
California Country Park
Finchampstead
Berkshire
RG40 4HT
Tel No: 0845 604 0414
www.reach-reading.demon.co.uk

Rifton
Jenx Limited
Wardsend Road
Sheffield
SE6 1RQ
Tel No: 0114 285 3376
Fax: 0114 285 3528
Email: info@jenx.com
www.jenx.com

Rompa International
Goyt Side Road
Chesterfield
Derbyshire
S40 2PH
Tel No: 01246 211 777
Fax: 01246 221 802
Email: sales@rompa.com
www.rompa.com

**Royal Association for Disability and
  Rehabilitation (RADAR)**
12 City Forum
250 City Road
London
EC1V 8AF
Tel No: 0207 250 3222
Fax No: 020 7250 0212
Email: radar@radar.org.uk
www.radar.org.uk

**Royal National Institute for the Blind
  (RNIB)**
105 Judd Street
London
WC1H 9NE
Tel No: 020 7388 1266
Fax No: 020 7388 2034
www.rnib.org.uk

**Royal National Institute for the Deaf
  (RNID)**
19–23 Featherstone Street

London
EC1Y 8SL
Tel No: 020 7296 8000
Fax No: 020 7296 8199
Email: informationline@rnid.org.uk
www.rnid.org.uk

Quest 88 Ltd
Aston Street
Shifnal
Shropshire
TF11 8DW
Tel No: 01952 463 050
Fax No: 01952 463 077
Email: sales@quest88.com
www.quest88.com

Quicktionary
Iansyst LTD
Fen House
Fen Road
Cambridge
CB4 1UN
Tel No: 01223 420 101
www.iansyst.co.uk

Scope
6–10 Market Road
London
N7 0PW
Tel No: 0808 800 3333 (Helpline)
www.scope.org.uk

SeeAbility
SeeAbility House
Hook Road
Epson
Surrey
KT19 8SQ
Tel No: 01372 755 000
Fax No: 01372 755 001
Email: enquiries@seeability.org
www.seeability.org

Soundabout
Thomley Barn
Menmarsh Road
Worminghall
HP18 9JZ
Tel No: 01844 338898
Email: info@soundabout.org.uk
www.soundabout.org.uk

SENSE
11–13 Clifton Terrace
Finsbury Park
London
N4 3SR
Tel No: 0207 272 7774
Fax No: 0207 272 6012
Email: info@sense.org.uk
www.sense.org.uk

Sherston Software Ltd
Angel House

Sherston
Malmesbury
Wiltshire
SN16 0LH
Tel No: 01666 843 200
Fax No: 01666 843 216
www.sherston.co.uk

Sickle Cell Society
54 Station Road
London
NW10 4UA
Tel No: 0208 961 7795
Fax No: 0181 961 8346
Email: info@sicktecellsociety.org
www.sicklecellsociety.org

Sight and Sound Technology
Qantel House
Anglia Way
Moulton Park
Northampton
NN3 6JA
Tel No: 01604 798070
        0845 634 7979
Fax No: 01604 798090
Email: sales@sightandsound.co.uk
www.sightandsound.co.uk

**Society for Mucopolysaccharide
    Disease**
MRS House
Repton Place
White Lion Road
Amersham
HP7 9LP
Tel No: 0845 3899902
Fax No: 0845 3899901
www.mpssociety.co.uk

SpaceKraft Ltd
Titus House
29 Saltaire Road
Shipley
West Yorkshire
BD18 3HH
Tel No: 01274 581 007
Fax No: 01274 531966
www.spacekraft.co.uk

TAC PAC
19 Florence Park Road
Oxford
OX4 3PN
Tel No: 01865 772213
Email: info@tacpac.co.uk
www.tacpac.co.uk

TAG Learning Ltd
25 Pelham Road
Gravesend
Kent
DA11 0HU
Tel No: 01474 357350
Fax No: 01474 537 887

Email: support@taglearning.com
www.taglearning.com

Techno-Vision Systems
76 Bunting Road
Industrial Estate
Northampton
NN2 6EE
Tel No: 01604 792 777
Fax No: 01604 792 726
Email: info@techno-vision.co.uk
www.techno-vision.co.uk

Thomson Software Solutions
74 Pine Grove
Brookmans Park
Hatfield
AL9 7BW
Tel No: 01707 654689
www.thomson-software-solutions.com

Teaching Handwriting Reading &
  Spelling Skills (Thrass)
Unit 1–3
Tarwin Sands
Barrow Lane
Tarwin
Chester
CH23 QS
www.thrass.co.uk

Toys for the Handicapped (TFH)
5–7 Severside Business Park
Stouport-On-Severn
Worchestershire
DY13 9HT
Tel No: 01299 827 820
Fax No: 01299 827 035
Email: tfh@tfhuk.com
www.tfhuk.com

Tyco Health Care
3 Elmwood
Chineham Business Park
Basingstock
Hants RG24 8WG
Tel No: 0125 6708880
www.tycohealthcare.com

Vari-tech Atkinson Engineering
Unit 4
Sett End Road
Shadsworth Business Park
Blackburn
BB1 2PT
Tel No: 01254 678777
Fax No: 01254 706 617

Widgit Software Ltd
124 Cambridge Science Park
Milton Road
Cambridge
CB4 OZS
Tel No: 01223 42558
Fax No: 01223 425 349
Email: sales@widget.com
www.widgit.com

Zychem Ltd
Valley Court
Sanderson Way
Middlewich
Cheshire
SW10 OGF
Tel No: 01606 738739
www.zychem.ltd.co.uk

Supporting Children Series

These books are ideal for both teachers and learning assistants in specialist and non-specialist settings. Each book provides theory about a specific need, plus practical advice, support and activities to facilitate children's learning.

Orders

All these titles are available from your local bookshop, but in the event of any difficulty please order directly from us.

Orca Book Services
Stanley House
3 Fleets Lane
Poole, Dorset
BH15 3AJ, UK

Tel: +44 (0) 1202 665 432
Fax: +44 (0) 1202 666 219
E-mail: orders@orcabookservices.co.uk

For ordering information inside North America, please call 1-800-561-7704.

(PHOTOCOPY AND USE)

SUPPORTING CHILDREN WITH ADHD

2nd Edition

Kate E. Spohrer

A collection of practical suggestions and materials to use with pupils who have ADHD or demonstrate ADHD-type behaviour. This new edition is enhanced by two new chapters: one on the theory, medication and alternative therapies for ADHD, and one covering what the teacher can do, including case studies, an Individual Education Plan (IEP) writing guide and reflective questions for the teacher about the child and teaching strategies.

May 2006 * 112pp * Paperback * A4
0 8264 8077 2 * **£17.50**

(PHOTOCOPY AND USE)

SUPPORTING CHILDREN WITH DYSLEXIA

2nd Edition

Garry Squires and Sally McKeown

Supporting Children with Dyslexia focuses on the practical difficulties facing dyslexic pupils every day in the classroom.

This second edition now offers even more information, particularly on the definitions of dyslexia, perceptual issues, spelling patterns, remedial programmes, useful techniques, and dyscalculia.

May 2006 * 160pp * Paperback * A4
0 8264 8078 0 * **£17.50**

(PHOTOCOPY AND USE)

SUPPORTING CHILDREN WITH SPEECH AND LANGUAGE IMPAIRMENT AND ASSOCIATED DIFFICULTIES

2nd Edition

Jill McMinn

This book describes how these difficulties can adversely affect children's learning in both specialist and mainstream settings and suggests how the curriculum can be made more accessible to facilitate learning.

This new edition has been fully updated and now includes a photocopiable, task-based assessment chapter, and a suggested structure for Individual Education Plans (IEP) together with a template and bank of possible targets.

May 2006 * 192pp * Paperback * A4
0 8264 9103 0 * **£20.00**

continuum

Continuum International Publishing Group Ltd • London and New York • www.continuumbooks.com